EMIL REM

— Stories of Loss, Redemption & Family —

EICA
PRESS

Book Design and Illustrations by Lorie Miller Hansen
Digital ePub design and creation by Andrea Cinnamond

9 781775 126669 >

First Edition, printed September 2022
www.EmilRem.ca   •   www.EICAPress.ca

"To the denizens of Manhattan…
for your overwhelming hospitality!"

—TABLE OF CONTENTS—

— FOREWORD —

Every author needs a sounding board. Mine came from a council of fifteen individuals who read each chapter as it came hot off the press and gave me their brutally frank opinions.

My first book, *Chasing Aphrodite,* is a travelogue sown with humour and love of a place that became my home-away-from-home every summer.

The second book is quite the opposite—gauging by the torrent of complaints received from my council.

Angry questions arose:

"Why are you writing about New York in mid-winter instead of sunny Cyprus?"

"Why are you comparing New York to Calgary, Canada?"

" Where are the descriptions of beautiful vistas we long for?"

Their questions were sprinkled with comments such as:

"So disappointing."

"Nothing like Aphrodite."

Some of the councillors suggested I hang up my hat on the laurels of my first book and retire while I still could.

Halfway through the book, one of them called me up, spending an hour to admonish me about Joe, one of my characters.

"Did you like him?" I asked.

"Of course not!"

"Then why are you wasting time discussing him?"

Little by little, it dawned on them that the book was not about exploring New York, but about the grey areas of right and wrong. It is a discussion of values and morals. Then, the penny dropped. Their enthusiasm began to gain the better of them. By the end, they were enthralled with *Heart of New York*.

To write such a book on the heels of *Chasing Aphrodite* was sheer lunacy. I loved Cyprus. It drew me back to my childhood. *Heart of New York* was another matter. My younger son forced me to go to New York because he was then a future rap artist and longed to visit his spiritual home. I wanted to return to Paradise Island, Bahamas, where we always spent Christmas.

New York greeted us with biting winds fresh off the Atlantic, restricting our every movement. The only vista we experienced was the pavement directly in front of us, which we scrutinized to avoid black ice—and one another's souls. Each venture out of our hotel was fog-bound and a battle against the snow and freezing rain. I felt like Captain Scott leading his party to inevitable doom.

Despite the misery surrounding us, the sunshine of hope and resilience pervaded every chapter, as a flower determined to bloom.

Emil

Emil Rem
Calgary, Alberta, September 11, 2022

"Did you ever see snow in Africa?"

CHAPTER 1
HEART OF NEW YORK

THE SNOW-FLAKED, fog-bound skyline of Manhattan loomed out at him as though through a powerful magnifying glass.

His family had been promised a suite from which they could *"experience the breath-taking vista of magnificent skyscrapers while sipping champagne from your balcony."* No skyline could be perceived. The giant buildings stood so terrifyingly close that they obliterated any sense of perspective. Through the swirling maelstrom, row-upon-row of offices soared to dizzying heights, bringing on such claustrophobia that he had to turn his back to retain his balance.

Why had he consented to come to this seemingly forlorn and inhospitable city? And at this time of the year?

Each Christmas, for a decade now, Paradise Island, Bahamas had beckoned his family to sunshine and warmth. A steel band welcomed them at Nassau airport, enthusiastically rattling out their favourite Christmas carols to a Caribbean beat. Ducking into the nearest washroom, they immediately abandoned their -40C winter garb for shorts, T-shirts and Crocs, which would sustain them over their two-week sojourn. The weather colluded, with warm 70F temperatures and cool tropical breezes culminating in perfect sweat-free harmony, day or night.

Christmas Eve was celebrated with a traditional Bahamian lunch buffet savoured at the British Colonial Hilton overlooking the palm-fringed, azure and turquoise sea with its flotilla of humungous cruise ships. They'd catch a ferry—a stone's throw away from the hotel—back to Paradise Island, then float on rafts down the lazy river that meandered through the island resort of Atlantis.

When they were boys, his two kids, Alex and Chris, loved the Bahamas as much as their own home in Calgary, Canada. But as they morphed into teenagers, rumblings of discontent grew ever louder.

"Bahamas? Not again? Why can't we go to New York for a change? That's where the action is." This from Chris, the younger of the two, now nicknamed "The Monster". He had blossomed from an unappetizing, continuously colicky baby into a fully-fledged hybrid Goth rapper with his spiritual Valhalla in Harlem.

"I thought you loved the Bahamas?" his father retorted. "Do you really want to spend Christmas snow-bound and stranded at LaGuardia airport?"

The Monster may have been a Goth rapper from hell, but he was a smart and accomplished conspirator. At the next family summit, his poor father was outvoted three to one in his bid for Christmas paradise.

Now here he was, tottering backwards into a comfy chair, over-powered by the giant edifices of Manhattan.

His reverie was interrupted by a storm of voices.

"Pops, my buddy Dinesh is here visiting with his mom and dad. Can we meet up?" the Monster asked in a syrupy tone.

"Pops, Saks has a sale on Armani leather jackets. The Book of Mormon is playing. Can we go?" his other son, "The Poodle" (named after his hairstyle— or rather the lack of it) glanced up from his laptop pointing to an "I Luv NY " website.

"Mum, where do you want to go?" Their voices rose in chorus.

"Bing's coming in by train from Boston. Can we pick her up at Grand Central Station?"

Laura's soft Filipina voice won the day. None in the family could refuse for fear of hurting her. Besides, Aunty Bing was their favourite.

"Don't forget your gloves and scarves!" Laura warned as they departed.

He peered at himself in the tall mirror by the door. Where were his shorts and T-shirt?" His oh-so-comfortable golden Crocs? He saw himself in black jogging pants and some old battered black Rockports—he still refused to wear winter boots. Instead of a down-filled winter jacket, he wore a hand-me-down leather jacket with a thin lining. Underneath he compensated with a chunky dark blue sweater to combat the cold. A bright orange and blue striped bobble hat crowned his head, always slipping upwards into a pointed cone before tumbling sideways to the ground, while his elastically-challenged jogging pants kept sliding down. He had forgotten his gloves.

Stepping out of the hotel onto Central Park Avenue, he could see nothing but fog and flakes of snow softly falling in slow motion accumulating like dandruff upon his shoulders. Suddenly, the weather changed—a howling wind bit into him. Lines of taxis across the road blocked any sight of the grand old park. Even the taxis could only be seen when they started up and their head-lights penetrated the fog.

"Let's take the subway," the boys said. In a flash, they were gone, and he was left clutching his wife to follow them into the void. He heard a clatter of clip-clops and almost ran headlong into a horse's face. Was he hallucinating? No. Horse-drawn carriages were operating tours across the park that he couldn't see.

The couple skidded to a halt at the entrance to the subway. The boys hurtled up the stairs towards them.

"Pops, the ticket machine's broken. We can't get in. We'll have to take a bus. Look, there's one." They pointed to a blue and white bus emerging through the fog, crunching to a halt.

The bus driver, a heavyset black woman, stared out at him through her thick, dark-framed glasses.

"Where's your MetroCard?" she insisted.

His family stood behind him in the biting wind and snow along with half-a-dozen passengers stamping their feet impatient to escape the winter blast.

"We don't have a card. The subway machine's broken. I have cash." He handed her some dollars.

"We don't take cash!" Her voice rose a significant decibel level.

Close to tears, the wind howling in his ears, he beat a retreat joining his family out on the street.

"Hey! Who told you to get off my bus?" she bellowed imperiously.

"But you said..." he snapped back.

"Come in and sit right there." She pointed to the handicapped seats behind her.

Confusion, despair, and her steely glare penned him in his seat. Passengers streamed past them in relief and the bus proceeded. It occurred to him that, in his haste to escape the cold, he didn't even know if they were on the right bus. He leaned forward hesitantly. "Excuse me, but are you going to Grand Central Station?"

"No. We go past it but don't stop." Her demeanour softened.

"Where are you folks from? Don't you know you need a Metro Card?" The driver glanced back at them just as she attempted a lane change. A deafening honk was heard within inches of them. She had almost bumped into a taxi. She remained unfazed, still waiting for an answer. His eyes surveyed his family. Laura seemed petrified. The Poodle had covered his face with his hands in embarrassment. The Monster glared at him. They had squeezed in beside what appeared to be a pre-revolution Russian dowager, wrapped from head to foot in plush brown fur, including her hat. She stiffened at the intrusion.

He smiled feebly at her. "We're from Canada. It's our first time here."

Still driving, she turned her head towards them. A fleeting smile lit her face. Was it his English accent, or the fact they were from Canada or motherly pity for his bedraggled family?

She stopped the bus in front of Grand Central. "Next time the machine's broken, knock on the office door beside it. Someone will come and help you." She moved to one side, reaching out her hand. "Here, take these." She handed them route maps and schedules of buses and the subway. She again waved him away when he offered to pay and vanished, along with her smile, into the maw of ongoing traffic.

Back outside, the bitter Atlantic wind assaulted them once again, reminding him of his first equally frigid winter in Calgary.

Each day he would stare out of the floor-to-ceiling window at the back of the ninth floor of Gulf Canada Square. Mile-long freight trains flew across the crisscrossed railway lines, puffing and bleating their way into the horizon with the wind and snow blowing every which way to slow them down. Why had he sought so cheerfully to leave England and, prior to that, Africa, to arrive at this Siberia of the North? BOREDOM.

At the age of twenty-four, he was a qualified Chartered Accountant with a well-paid and respectable career ahead of him. Did he really want to spend the rest of his life commuting to London from his suburban home? A path, routine and predictable, lay in front of him with an obligatory maisonette and gold watch at the end of it. He was single and craving adventure when an ad enticed him to apply, partly as a joke, to an accounting firm in Canada. A place called Calgary—a queer juxtaposition of "Cowtown" and modern oil boom with a Scottish name endowed upon it by its querulous Calvinist founding fathers.

"You're mad!" His all-knowing mother expostulated.

"But it's the fastest growing city in Canada. It's swimming in oil."

Recent years in England had been an economic nightmare. Margaret Thatcher had waged war on unions and specifically coalminers in Wales leading to unremitting strikes, riots and blackouts amid blizzards and deep snow—dubbed The Winter of Discontent. In training, he had accompanied his manager to Wales, Sheffield and Gateshead to close down coal mines and steelworks where proud and tradition-bound workers were forever discarded on the rubbish heap of redundancy. There had to be a better place to work and live. Somewhere with a boundless future.

"You can't even make up your own bed." Her last words of admonishment to him before he boarded the plane for the seven-hour flight.

He was now a "Team Leader" with a glass-fronted office facing a bullpen of carrels full of trainees to assist him in managing the accounting assignments of his employer, Collins Barrow, Chartered Accountants.

Instead of a dingy, smelly English attic sharing a large oak table with three other incumbents, he was privy to an air-controlled grey oasis of sterile loneliness equipped with a standard desk, one reclining chair and a single bookcase identical to his neighbour—every action formalized, any deviance strictly proscribed.

One gloomy day, eaten up with remorse at his chosen life path, he rebelled.

From a storage room of broken and discarded furniture, he borrowed a coffee table —a sin beyond redemption in the eyes of his colleagues. Onto it he emptied a 5,000-piece jigsaw puzzle. His wayward action brought nothing but dismay and consternation to his fellow inmates. Was it the jigsaw puzzle itself or the fact that it was all red that caused the furore? He couldn't tell. His action cemented their notion of how wrong the management was in recruiting such an oddball. And all the way from England too!

"Old Collins won't like it," Gary, a colleague, whispered to him, unsure of how to break this precious intelligence to him.

Mr. John Ewart Collins was the bane of the office, the senior partner of the firm his English father had founded. Tall and beefy, he barely spoke yet exuded a whiff of disapproval in his wake whenever he stepped out of his office to consult his minions.

A day later, the reckoning came in the form of a knock on his door. It was the boss himself.

"Is that yours?" Collins pointed to the puzzle.

"Yes." He answered in a panic.

"Well, it's a mess."

"Sorry, sir. I'll clear it up." He began to box the pieces.

Collins eyed him thoroughly. "You've got it all wrong."

"Pardon?"

"To do this properly, you must sort the pieces into groups, not pile them into heaps. Look..."

One minute he was standing up, his six-foot-six frame blocking the glass front of the office. The next, he was on his knees sorting out the pieces into straight ends and rows of similar-shaped pieces, like a child playing with his favourite box of Lego bricks.

"We do this every Christmas at home. To do it right, you have to be organized and methodical. Like an accountant."

An hour passed. Staff walking by at their usual brisk pace stopped sharply and about-turned. Some brought their colleagues to witness the spectacle.

At noon, John Collins asked if he cared to join him for lunch. Passing the window overlooking the train lines now obliterated by the swirling snow, the boss remarked "You came from Africa, didn't you? Did you ever see snow there?"

"Yes sir, at the movies." He smiled impishly.

The weather in New York had grown ever colder, ever wetter, yet a large grin plastered his face as he remembered Old Collins. His family stared at him in bewilderment as, for once, he led them through crowd-beset Park Avenue to enter Grand Central Station.

AUTHOR'S NOTE

Nudging the Prism

A bellicose bus driver, a daunting senior partner—suddenly the light changes and their other facets are revealed.

Do we spend too long staring at the one colour people emanate, forgetting the rest of their spectrum?

It's time to nudge the prism.

ILLUSTRATOR'S NOTE

A whirlwind of excitement and trepidation—leaving behind everything familiar for the thrill of the unknown (or barely known)—racing toward what waits on the other side of the world!

"Even the auditors loved him... at first."

CHAPTER 2
BARNEY BARRACUDA

THE VENERABLE JW Marriot Essex House stood on an avenue abounding in five-star glitzy hotels, all lumped together at the foot of Central Park.

The unmistakable Plaza Hotel stood close by, with flags of every nation jutting onto the avenue horizontally, with hot-dog and roasted chestnut vendors hustling for business. A few steps on towards Columbus Circle, Essex House rose unassuming, passersby never giving it a glance. Observed from across the street to gain a true perspective, the 44-storey edifice would not have looked out of place beside the magnificent architecture running along the length of Central Park to Harlem. Essex House retained its anonymous discretion until the observer reached its summit, where, in garish, bright red two-storey high letters, it proclaimed its name to the world.

Walking in from the miserable snow-rain mess of the avenue, his family was immediately ensconced in an atmosphere of warm welcome.

Black and white diamond-shaped tiles covered its floors. Two 9-foot Christmas trees decked with balls and baubles, seemingly plucked from the nineteenth century, stood like sentries on each side of the lobby. The wrapped "presents" stacked haphazardly underneath drew him helplessly back to his Christmases with his English foster family—he, as a child peeping surreptitiously at the gifts, pondering which were destined for him. The only thing missing was the angel doll upon the tree. Flo, his foster mother, had sewn her in sparkling white taffeta giving her a home-made wand to bestow wishes of goodwill on all who gazed up at her.

The hotel staff were wholesome and naturally accommodating, much to his chagrin. He missed his Christmas in the Bahamas, soaking up the sun beside an endless pool of water, not fighting the wind, snow, and rain in New York. He was determined to find fault and prove his family wrong in coming here.

He picked up the phone. "Housekeeping, we've bought some cereals and milk for breakfast. Do you have any bowls and spoons we could use?" He knew it was against hotel protocol which preferred to promote its own restaurant and room service instead.

"Of course, sir. We'll deliver them right away. How many sets would you like?"

As he raised his eyebrows and wordlessly replaced the phone on its cradle, his family watched him, probably regretting bringing him along. He pretended not to notice, raising the phone yet again, this time directing his call to the concierge. "We'd love a helicopter ride over Manhattan." He winked at his family in their deluded Christmas cheer.

"When would you like to go? We can have a limousine drive you to the helipad. I'll send some brochures up immediately."

Before he could decline, the concierge hung up the phone. Damn, it was now going to cost him another tip for the bell-boy. Why was everything "immediate" or "right away"? Why couldn't they behave like every other hotel? He could hear the "Monster", his younger son, sniggering in the background.

Next, he returned to housekeeping. "We love your weighing scale. Can we buy one from you to take back to Canada?" He expected to be directed to a useless website and had his pen and paper handy.

Minutes later, a brand-new model, replete with a blue screen displaying weights in three different measures: pounds, stones and kilograms landed at their door with the note "With our compliments. Merry Christmas." No charge.

With renewed vigour, he took the elevator down to reception where he faced his next adversary: a mere strip of a girl, barely five-foot-tall, Chinese, with finely structured bones and a face like delicate porcelain. In rapt silence she listened to his concern. "My sister-in-law and her husband are stranded here for a couple of days because of bad weather. Would you have a spare room for them?"

There was no way at Christmastime and with the weather delaying flights and cancelling train schedules that the hotel would have any space. His own family had to book months in advance.

"Yes sir, we do have a room for them. We always set aside two suites at Christmas for such contingencies." She smiled at him as though he was her best friend, annihilating the last of his resistance.

While bowed in defeat, he closed his eyes and the heart-warming smile of Barney Barracuda (aka Barney Baratelli) came down to taunt him.

Back in Calgary, Canada many decades earlier, when he had emigrated from England to work with Collins Barrow, Chartered Accountants, Monday morning team meetings were held at 8.30 a.m. sharp.

One winter morning as he walked the five blocks to his office, dressed in an Inuit-style goose-down Hudson's Bay parka, he had covered his head with a scarf and a hood edged in fur. The bright sunshine and clear blue sky had made the -40C weather deceptively inviting but deadly if you weren't dressed adequately. Mere minutes of exposure of any part of your skin led to frostbite or worse. He walked with clumsy, robot-like steps. As the air entered his hood it turned to mist against his glasses and froze, making them opaque. Wearing inch-thick gloves he couldn't take off, he hazarded his way along the streets, blind, confused and cold. Fifteen minutes later, when he still hadn't reached his office, he removed his hood and glasses to find his bearings only to discover he had overshot his target and was even further away from his office than when he had started out.

He barged into the oversized boardroom, still in his parka and Arctic gloves, tottered to the nearest empty chair, half an hour late. The meeting of twenty people shuddered to a halt.

John Collins, the senior partner glared at him, starting in with a list of questions.

"Have you touched base with Mrs. Ryder?" The boss stood in front of a blackboard, pointing his chalk at him, while the next in line to be questioned studied their notes anxiously.

Coming from England, he had no clue of baseball idioms. "I've even scored a home run, but to no avail." He meant that after several calls he had finally got her, but she still hadn't prepared the information he needed. Several snickers and a guffaw escaped before they were silenced by Collins.

"How is the audit of Westwinds Hotel coming along with Gary? Wasn't it supposed to have finished last week?" He looked from Gary back to him.

Meanwhile, his discarded parka was dripping water onto a chair and part of the conference table and his boots had left a stain on the expensive blue-grey plush carpet.

Gary attempted a rescue but failed miserably. "Sir, I think we've discovered a fraud."

A hush fell over the room. All eyes focussed on them. Gary began to twitch.

To this day, even in the lobby of the Essex, he could feel his heart pounding, see those eyes riveted upon him and John Collins hovering above.

The Asian receptionist's million-dollar smile had transformed into a frown of concern. "Is there anything else we can do for you? Would you like me to summon the porter to carry any luggage?" He stared at her as though in a trance.

In the heyday of Calgary's oil boom, two rival families, both prominent clients of Collins Barrow, had joined hands to purchase the Westwinds. The plan was to knock down the hotel and replace it with an office tower. To avoid being gazumped, the offer to purchase was presented in a flash before a partnership agreement could be executed. And the property was owned equally.

Three years later, with still no agreement in place, a son of one of the families was left in charge of the hotel with absolutely no experience in the business. Collins Barrow had been hired to perform an annual audit to satisfy the other partner. Neither wanted to pay the exorbitant price of an audit.

As Collins and the rest of the team stared at them, he could guess what they were thinking.

Some kook from England with his local sidekick, both just recently hired, were two weeks over budget, already doubling the audit fee. Their excuse, the discovery of a fraud that no one at Collins Barrow had found in the past three years of auditing.

"I want you both in my office immediately. This meeting is over."

Despite being the senior partner, Collins's office was no bigger than their own. But at least it had a window. One wall was covered with obligatory certificates and citations along with framed photos of Collins receiving awards and shaking hands with celebrities and businessmen. There was a photo of Collins with the recent mayor, Rod Sykes, who also happened to be a chartered accountant. Even in his trepidation, he glanced over at the boss's desk to catch a glimpse of a family photo. There was none.

In one corner stood a round table, three-feet in diameter, with four chairs circling it. From its centre rose a magnificent dark bronze statue of a rodeo cowboy clinging to a bucking horse: one hand held high gripping his hat and the other desperately clutching his horse's reins.

As they sat down, Collins asked, "Gary, explain to me how you came about this "fraud"?"

Still twitching, Gary let loose a dry cough and began.

"Z-tapes, sir. We were examining samples from the cash tills. Each transaction should have a specific sequential number. In one of our sample batches, the till roll at the end of the day had been torn off, removing several transactions. Examining further, we found more missing. There were gaps in the sequence between the end of one day and the beginning of the next."

"How many did you find? Over what period?" The boss began to show more sympathy.

"Several and regularly over the year. We discovered a pattern." Gaining confidence, Gary ploughed on. "The missing transactions were always on a weekend. The only person working those shifts was Barney Baratelli."

Barney, the ever-smiling, over-accommodating high chamberlain of the Westwinds began his career as a busboy when the 60-room hotel opened twenty years before. Through unstinting loyalty and an unquenchable desire to take on the least desirable shifts in the hotel, the "Barracuda" (a play on his surname used by the auditors between themselves as the investigation proceeded) had risen to chief adviser and confidant to the new owner/manager. There was nothing Barney wouldn't do for him. Meanwhile, the rest of the staff adored Barney for the personal interest he took in them.

Even the auditors loved him.... at first. When there was no parking, Barney would have a reserved spot waiting for them. He commandeered a suite for them to operate from. "The hotel office is too small for you," he would always say. Barney brought them mid-morning snacks, their favourite newspapers and afternoon teas.

Barney would do the same for guests attending high society weddings and other functions. Too drunk to venture home, they turned to their friend Barney to find them a room in the jam-packed hotel. In pre-credit card days, guests paid in cash to avoid the hassle and any detection through the use of cheques. These transactions were always late at night.

"How come the audit is taking so long this year?" he asked them one day.

"Oh, new audit procedures."

"You're taking away all your files every day. Why not leave them in your suite? Saves the lugging. I'll keep the key and make sure no one enters without me." A shiver ran down their backs as the two auditors looked at each other. How long could this go on for?

It turned out that the Barracuda pocketed at least $20,000, ripped off the last segments of the Z-tapes and went home at dawn smiling to himself and, over the years making hundreds of guests ever grateful to him until the auditors began to have their doubts.

A month later, it all came to a head. Gary was driving them to report to their client. The boss's New Yorker was in for service, so they were all packed into Gary's battered and grey Riviera. The six-foot Collins squished into the front passenger seat, his knees bumping his chin.

"Don't say a word. I'll do the talking," admonished their boss, as they pulled into their reserved spot at the hotel.

"What do you mean it's Barney? That's impossible!" The owner gesticulated with shock and horror. "What am I going to do without him?" There was a moment of silence as he pondered the full significance of Collins's report. Then he rose up defiantly from his chair. "Who told you to spend all this time on the audit?"

Collins was at their defence immediately. "If you read our engagement letter, our duty is to pursue any and every test if we come across a suspicion of fraud. We have to establish there really was a fraud, not just a gross error. And we need to establish irrefutable proof of the culprit. This fraud was practiced regularly and for many years and amounted to way over the stipulated $5,000 legal minimum."

He paused to take a deep breath. "Our initial samples were small and random, which explains why we didn't come across this in previous years. You should be grateful to our team." Collins glanced over at him and Gary.

The owner/manager stared back at Collins as if he was crazy. In a quivering voice he asked, "What's going to happen now? How do we explain this to our partner? What about the publicity? Where am I going to find another Barney?"

Between the Christmas trees devoid of their taffeta angel, upon the black and white spotless diamond squared floor, he stood rooted until the Chinese receptionist came out to him, gently tapping his shoulder. "Is there anything else you need, sir?"

No there wasn't, only a reprieve from a "Barracuda" smile that haunted him each time he stepped into a hotel lobby.

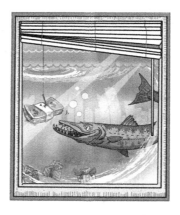

AUTHOR'S NOTE

Appeasing the Fish

The English language may describe a fish as a large, predatory marine beast with a slender body and large jaws and teeth—however, fish can also be prison slang for new first-time inmates (usually considered naive and vulnerable) who'd better learn quickly.

A description of the perpetrator, his victim, or us?

ILLUSTRATOR'S NOTE

What's really going on underneath the surface? That "great guy", someone you rely on, someone you think you know—is really preying on everyone's good will and naiveté to line his own pockets—a hungry barracuda eating up all the little fishes' food!

"They looked around and couldn't see him."

CHAPTER 3

THE MAYOR COMES
TO TOWN

THERE WAS NO sound of Christmas... only a perpetual thud to his eardrums as they descended the grimy, concrete steps of the New York subway to Battery Park. The noise grew ever louder as they neared their platform. His gait stiffened. He almost raised his hands to muffle his ears from the din.

"Relax Pops, it's Techno music." Chris smiled, trying to re-assure him.

As they approached the vortex of this cacophony, it appeared they had entered the backstage of a rock show. Gyrating dancers, a manic drummer and musicians pressing onto hand-held keyboards that he had never seen before heightened his dismay. So, this was the Big Apple's version of Silent Night.

The circus continued on the train. Although at this time, there were few passengers on board (being way past rush hour), the corridors were lined with kids somersaulting and break dancing to boom boxes he hadn't seen since his school days. The show was stunning, with the inevitable call for cash at its conclusion. Other youths, not even in their teens, handed out pocket-sized boxes of cereals in expectation of dollar bills, not coins.

Curiously, they didn't faze or intimidate him. He had spent too many Christmases in the Bahamas catching small ferry boats from Paradise Island to Nassau and back. Each trip would cost $4 US. A 'guide' would also embark, walking around the boat spouting information to the thirty-odd passengers about the sites passed along the journey at the end of which, he would pass a baseball cap around expecting donations.

Despite himself, he found the New York cereal boys charming, though he wondered what they would do when they grew up... if they grew up.

His family was on their way to the ferry terminals to see the Statue of Liberty and board their prearranged helicopter ride over the island of Manhattan.

As usual, as they disembarked at their destination, the boys rocketed off, only to return all forlorn.

"Pops, they've cancelled all flights due to bad weather," they chorused, looking at him for direction. He, in turn, sighed with inner relief. This whole escapade was a result of his ongoing tussle with their hotel. He, unhappy to spend Christmas in New York, had continued to make ever higher demands on the staff to prove their shortcomings. It culminated in him asking for a helicopter ride. He had never intended to go—only to harass the staff.

Since childhood, he had suffered severe motion sickness on Ferris wheels, let alone in swooping helicopters. But, the whole family, even Laura, jumped at the idea with such enthusiasm that he could find no real excuse to refuse.

"How about the United Nations Headquarters?" he suggested. "It's down the road." His family acceded. Anything to escape the brutish weather.

The ten-minute walk felt like an hour's trek across the Arctic—the wind and snow a constant.

At the entrance gate, a heavily armed soldier warded them off. "Tickets? You can't enter without them."

It turned out you could only buy the tickets online and weeks in advance to gain security clearance.

New York's infamous winter pursued them relentlessly like the Russians harrying Napoleon from Moscow.

They came back to the ferry and took a selfie in front of the Statue of Liberty. From his perspective, it was tiny. As they herded together to fit into the frame, all that remained of Madame Liberty was her torch atop his head.

They carried on to Wall Street. The thoroughfare was smaller than he expected and jam-packed with people. The buildings—Georgian townhouses—appeared to have been transplanted from a cul-de-sac in Bath, England, even to the very cobbled road laid out in front of them, clearly not the image he had always had of towering skyscrapers overwhelming him in every direction.

An oversized bronze bull stood in the centre of the road rearing its head, confronting a little girl in bronze a couple of feet away.

The street teemed with suited proteges carrying pencil-thin

briefcases, cell phones glued to their ears, their black gabardine coats wide open and their woollen scarves dancing in the wind, impervious to the cold. Hordes of tourists, draped in haute couture, lumbered around like Visigoths at the fall of Rome, hauling away their precious loot in large heavy paper carrier bags emblazoned with logos of the most exclusive brands in the world, scrupulously avoiding the 'bums' hunched forward on their knees begging for reprieve.

Bedraggled and numb, soaked to the bone, he led his family through a maze of alleys and truncated streets unsure of what he was looking for—perhaps a glimpse of the last remnant of a local community or the wizened architecture of a bygone era.

Choosing back streets away from the glitz and swank, he sought solace... and found it in a forest of white oaks which emptied onto a chest-high wall surrounding a square acre of land.

The trees numbed the sound of traffic and lent an air of serenity to their quest. Chris and Alex slowed down. A spate of silence overwhelmed them as they reached out to touch the wall and peer over it.

The wall was of grey-black basalt crowned in bronze. Upon that bronze were etched the names of thousands. Water flowed noiselessly from the top, gently towards a square black void at its epicentre. The pool glistened and the water, moving so gently, lulled him into a sense of calm and reflection.

He realised he was standing on the very spot the World Trade Center had once stood.

Like everyone else in the world, that September morning and the very many mornings thereafter were seared upon his memory. It was a Tuesday and he was driving himself to a breakfast meeting. As usual, he turned on the radio to CBC 1010 AM.

"The World Trade Center has been hit by a plane." Minutes later, a second explosion and still no certainty of its cause. Apocalyptic news of a plane crash near the Pentagon.

Switching off the radio, he entered Humpty's Restaurant. Four television screens ran what seemed to be a King Kong movie in technicolour. But why were they running the same scene over and over again?

He found his client in a huddle of strangers in front of a TV set. Someone had cranked the volume to full.

Days were filled with the continuous loop of a thirty second strip from someone's camera. Blurred images came in and out of focus—individuals shot out of a universe of fire and blinding dust in a mad dash to escape. As survivors catapulted themselves out of danger, firemen, police, paramedics and common citizens, without masks or protective clothing, hurled themselves back into the fray to salvage whatever lives they could. Later, men caked in dust returned abjectly from the scene, defeated in their quest. Their faces beyond tears.

Beyond the brain-numbing images of planes crashing into office towers, he remembered one above all: President George W. Bush sitting in a classroom of preschool kids, a giant straddling one of their tiny chairs with a book of fairy tales open in front of him—his face never betraying the news being whispered into his ear. The news clip robbed of all sound. Then there was New York's Mayor Giuliani rallying everyone.

A few years later, Mr. Giuliani came to Calgary as a keynote speaker for a fundraising event. He remembered the NYC Mayor in an immaculately pressed suit and dazzling white shirt and the forceful, jingoistic thrust of his manner and speech... so different from the breakfast meeting for Naheed Nenshi, the first Muslim Mayor of Calgary.

A friend, a director of Calgary Economic Development, had called him. "We have an American Ismaili Muslim business delegation visiting us for a week. Can you act as host? You're an Ismaili and a local businessman."

"What do you want me to do with them? I haven't been to a mosque in decades. I'm married to a Filipina and my kids are Roman Catholic."

"Just show up at the Glenbow on Monday...and wear a suit."

The last time he had worn a suit was at a wedding years earlier. All he ever wore now were jogging pants and a hoodie.

"And be there by 8.30 a.m. to greet everyone before Mayor Nenshi arrives at nine."

Forty people packed the room. Each wore their best suit or dress and sat down promptly at 8.55 a.m., full of anticipation to receive our new Mayor who was one of their own—an Ismaili.

9 a.m. came and passed. At 9.30 a.m. delegates looked at each other and glanced at their Rolexes and Piagets. A female executive in a sheer black skirt and Ferragamo jacket twiddled with her white pearl necklace in exasperation. An hour later, as they collectively exhausted their texting, someone announced the arrival of his Worship the Mayor.

They looked around and couldn't see him.

A diminutive figure stood before them. He was wearing a grey and brown Argyll sweater with balls of fluff hanging out from all sides. It looked like it had been salvaged from a thrift store. He was unshaven. Strands of hair ran upwards in streaks as though he had forgotten to comb his hair.

The delegates looked aghast. They glanced at each other, comparing wordless notes. Was this a joke?

"Sorry for being late. I just got back from Disneyland."

The hostility in the room could have been set on fire. Was this really the Mayor? The man they had come all this way to see? Only his skin colour could support that assumption.

Glancing from the Mayor to his audience, he shook his head in disbelief. The whole tour, including this meeting, had been choreographed for months and to the minute. In one sentence, the Mayor had thrown a bomb into the works. His neck began to itch uncontrollably in its effort to break loose from his tight shirt collar.

His Worship continued, addressing an audience who had paid thousands of dollars each to be there with the potential to invest millions in his city.

"Every year, we take kids to Disneyland as part of the 'Make A Wish Foundation' for terminally sick children. Our sponsors can only fly us out at four in the morning and then return us the same time the next day. Unfortunately, we were delayed at L.A. airport for several hours. I also had to stop at a high school on the way here to give out awards to students for outstanding service to their community."

For a moment, the female executive stopped twirling her pearl necklace. A number of her colleagues who had been furiously tapping at their smart phones, as if in the midst of emailing their complaints to the organizer, also stopped and looked up.

His Worship gave an ad lib speech of welcome. If his oratory stirred any of his congregation, they showed no sign of it.

Mayor Naheed Nenshi shook hands, accepted a gift, then

participated in a group photo session and promptly left, never once acknowledging their common connection to Islam.

He sat in a stupor as the Mayor exited the floor. His feelings towards him swung back and forth like a pendulum. Why hadn't His Worship made the most of this opportunity to trumpet his religious and social connection to his audience? Didn't he care? Why hadn't he spent more time glad-handing the crowd? After all he was a politician. Something was missing. For the life of him, he just couldn't connect with him.

A year after the U.S. delegation left town, his father died. A month later, as was custom, he came to his grave to pay respect. His father had been buried in a lonely corner of the Garden of Peace on the outskirts of town. The acreage of land was so new that not a fence broke the view of the endless prairie. A boundless blue sky came to greet it at the tip of the farthest horizon.

The bitter wind slapped his face. There was no shelter to turn to. In accordance with Ismaili ritual, a josh stick had to be lit and planted in front of his father's headstone to purify the air and ward off evil spirits.

There was no headstone, only a slab of granite two feet by one, laid flat upon his father's grave. Trying for the umpteenth time to light a match to ignite the josh stick, a hand came out of nowhere to cup the flame.

It was Mayor Nenshi standing beside him.

Both their fathers had died within days of each other and were buried side by side. Their two children had come and gathered here on a peaceful Sunday afternoon without pomp and circumstance to pay them homage on a lonely patch of ground so many continents away from their homeland in Africa. The Mayor had lent him a hand while no one else was watching.

Above the memorial in New York, the sun escaped the clouds to lighten the sky, yet the wind cut through the trees, knifing the water.

Save for the smothered hum of the city and the twittering of some renegade birds, all was still, including his silent, downcast family. For that moment in time, each had withdrawn into their own world. Wetting her fingers in the water, his wife sought further benediction in crossing herself with them.

As he faced the parapet bearing the names of thousands, he wondered what task each of them had been set to accomplish that day and, whether they too had been given an unexpected hand in their final moments.

AUTHOR'S NOTE

Divesting the Allegory

Did anyone catch the allegory of the perceived Canadian way of practising world diplomacy—(Nenshi) contrasted to the American (Giuliani)?

The endless ramifications of a chosen policy—yet another perpetrator of 9/11 blown up while luxuriating in a protective haven.

Or seeking a lonely benediction amid the knifing wind of a New York City winter?

ILLUSTRATOR'S NOTE

The cold loneliness of a windy prairie sky is used as the physical manifestation for the feeling of losing a loved one, and a simple, unexpected act of compassion can have all the warmth of the sun in that moment.

"... Besides, the stories were funny."

CHAPTER 4

BAND OF ANGELS

AT ALMOST ONE o'clock in the afternoon, his family was still sound asleep after attending the opening midnight showing of *Into the Woods* with Meryl Streep at a cinema around the corner. That left him a couple of hours to himself. He peered out the window of their hotel at the gigantic skyscrapers of Manhattan invading the light. Thankfully the snow had stopped.

He stepped out of Essex House, bid Frank the bellboy (in his seventies) a "good afternoon" and turned left towards Columbus Circle. Finally, no biting wind to fight through and the sun shone brightly above Central Park across the road. Cars flew back and forth cutting through slush and mud.

In the week he'd been there, the surrounding area had become his parish. He remembered Petrossian and took a detour. Two brothers, Melcoum and Mouchegh, refugees from Armenia had founded their first store in Paris in 1920. They established trading relations with Russia and specialised in caviar and spices. He came for their French pastries that melted in his mouth. If the weather cooperated, he would eat them in the Park.

As usual, there was a lineup. The recent inclement weather had done nothing to improve his health. He was wheezing and coughing into the crook of his elbow when the lady behind him proffered a Kleenex. Then, from the depths of a cavernous pocket in her fur coat, she fished out a tin of cough drops and offered him one.

"Every Saturday, I come here from Brooklyn for my order of smoked salmon. They fly it in from Paris." She looked as majestic as the building—Alwyn Court—they were in. Built in the French Renaissance style, the entire facade was made up of elaborate terracotta, like a poorer neighbour of Notre Dame Cathedral.

He bowed his head in gratitude, too scared to start a conversation for fear of his hacking cough. Once started, it wouldn't stop.

Finally, it was his turn to be served. Expecting a nubile pretty young thing in a severe black uniform, he was approached by a centenarian, in a blouse of brilliant colours: azure blue, budgerigar yellow and fuchsia pink—her body stooped forward almost in a vee shape.

"Can I help you, sir?"

He wheezed out his order and she didn't miss a beat. He wasn't sure what startled him the most, her age, appearance, or the brilliant smile that she bestowed upon him as she took his money. Forgetting himself, he smiled back with equal warmth, carting his large paper carrier bag of goodies out of the store.

Walking past Carnegie Hall, he rested for a moment. Since he was a child, he had been in love with classical music. Where he had gotten this love from confounded his English working-class family. His favourite adverts on television included the one for Benson and Hedges cigars. A man wrapped entirely in bandages was spectating a tennis match. As soon as he had managed to turn his whole head in the direction of the ball, the ball had been hit back to the opposite end of the court. Perpetually playing catch up, he gave up and asked his companion to light him a mini cigar and he found bliss, accompanied by Bach's 'Air on the G String'. Adverts were followed by news shows such as 'This Week'. Its theme music (and the first classical LP he bought) was the 'Karelia Suite' by Jean Sibelius. Later, he bought an LP record (and later a CD) of Vladimir Horowitz, giving his first piano recital at this very building.

He hummed a few bars of *The Great Gate of Kiev* to himself as he proceeded to the basement of Time Warner Center—a few blocks away—to shop for groceries.

The Whole Foods store sprawled across the entire basement. Until now, he had always been disappointed with the quality of produce in America compared to Canada. The United States was great for gigantic, foot-cube boxes of Pepperidge Farm Goldfish crackers akin to the Peek Freans Cheeselets he used to devour in England.

He picked up some Danone fruit yoghurt and sugar-free Mesa Sunrise cereal, skim milk and bananas—all of which his kids would detest. He bumped his trolley into individuals of every race and colour, all wearing clothes with their high-end brands clearly marked. A few days ago, he had made the mistake of arriving here at six in the evening. The emporium was chock-a-block with office staff spewing out of the surrounding towers, ordering nutritious takeout meals from the in-store deli.

Coming off the escalator onto the main lobby, he shouldered his way through the revolving doors and winked at Columbus sitting atop his perch on a column at the centre of a traffic island, surrounded by driving savages. Welcome to the New World.

Waiting for a gap in the traffic, he glanced at his watch. There was still time to visit John.

Darting through the battlefield of warring vehicles, he took a weaving path in some nondescript corner of Central Park until he came to a Portuguese-style circular mosaic in white and grey tiles with the word Imagine at its centre.

The size and shapes of landmarks in Manhattan always baffled him. Expecting large and brash, neon flashing signs to show the way, he was disappointed to see this barely nine-foot diameter, the size of his family's round dining table, stuck in the middle of a winding pathway as a memorial to John Lennon. Then again, in all his ramblings across this breathtakingly beautiful and tranquil park, he had never seen a memorial to any US President.

He sat down on a bench and took out a Petrossian croissant to nibble, and a bouquet of memories came to him.

On the 28th of April, 1980 he emigrated to Calgary, Canada from England. It took six months to build a credit record before he could lease a television from Granada TV Rental. One of the first news items he watched was John Lennon's assassination on December 8—a date he couldn't forget, because it was his father's birthday and later, his son's.

The music of John and the Beatles had punctuated so many of his formative years. Going to Africa in summer, he listened to 'Eight Days a Week' on the radio each Sunday from the local

Top of the Pops countdown. That song made number one for two whole years.

In England, he was given his first LP—A Hard Day's Night—on his ninth birthday. On his twelfth birthday, his mother gave him his first portable cassette recorder and player, as heavy as a safe, the length of an egg carton and twice as wide. His first recording was All You Need is Love—a musical rage at the time, blending classical music with pop.

Central Park buzzed with activity. Strangers came and sat beside him for a minute and walked away, their attention fixed on the mosaic and their own thoughts. They were promptly replaced by others. Meanwhile, the sun shone ever brighter.

He had recently spent a couple of days in Liverpool. "You must take a London cab tour of all the Beatles' haunts," exhorted the captivating, petite, blonde receptionist. He couldn't refuse her.

As the driver cruised past Strawberry Field (not Fields), an orphan home whose grounds John would play in, the taxi boomed its tribute to the Fab Four. They had a break in a church graveyard where John would skive off from school to smoke a cigarette or two. The guide pointed to the grave of Eleanor Rigby.

Rain streamed down as they navigated Penny Lane, a bus terminal where the four boys met before deciding whose home they should go to. Nearly all the shops referred to on the record still existed. The characters mentioned were all real too, according to his guide.

The grand finale—a row of council houses where Paul McCartney had lived as a boy and where John wrote songs with him.

The post-World War II homes made of flint and stone brought

tears to his eyes. They were identical to the home he was raised so many years ago in Ellington Park in North Maidenhead, Berkshire, thirty miles south of London.

In front of the homes, he saw coach-upon-coach parked one behind the other, in a narrow, one lane cul-de-sac. Out poured hundreds of Asian tourists led by flag-waving guides shouting in Cantonese, Mandarin and Japanese (so far as he could recognize), all storming into this little home as though they were charging onto a Cathay Pacific plane on its first boarding announcement.

This brought further tears to his eyes, wondering what it would feel like if they overran his old home in Ellington Park.

Back at the memorial, someone stepped on his toe. "Oh, so sorry." A young Asian woman, walking backwards into him apologized in a thick accent. She was taking a photo with her iPhone of her friend contorting her body to one side to get herself, the whole mosaic and the footpath leading to it, all into one shot. And, of course, as in virtually every photo shoot he had witnessed across Asia, the girl was conjuring up a 'V' sign over the inscription Imagine.

He looked up at the sky. It was darkening and he was late returning to the hotel and his expectant family.

Entering their suite, Laura was taking a shower. In the sitting room, the boys were playing Civilization on their laptop, evidently enjoying the day's break from sightseeing.

Apparently, no one had missed him. "Hurry up. We're late," he said in a huff.

Bundled up and sweating in their winter garb, the whole family charged out of the hotel and, this time, turned right toward Bloomingdales, an hour before closing time on Christmas Eve.

Halfway to their destination, he stopped dead in his tracks staring into a shop window: the name H*Y*M*A*N K*A*P*L*A*N stared back at him like a flashing neon sign.

"You guys go ahead. I'll meet you there."

The Argosy Book Store on 59th Street reeled him in, not with a siren call but with the only book title that would have drawn him like iron filings to a magnet. An exhibition of Hyman Kaplan books by Leonard Q. Ross, the pen name of Leo Rosten, displayed in its window. He entered an Aladdin's cave of rare and precious books, a pantheon of the world's most renowned authors. To him, after trawling second-hand bookstores for a lifetime, it was like entering the Louvre to gain an audience with Mona Lisa.

Remarkably, there was no sign of dust. No musty smell. The antiseptic wooden bookshelves seemed to have been polished daily. A framed and signed photograph of Ernest Hemingway stood on a stand, presumably for sale.

In Africa, as a teenager, he had been given a book token and promptly cashed it in for two volumes by Alan Moorehead entitled *The Blue Nile* and *The White Nile*. Here they were, in pristine first editions.

His iPhone-toting kids would never have understood his sentimentality, which is why he had sent them on to Bloomingdales with Laura.

Grabbing the nearest Kaplan book, he anxiously explored its pages. Yes, it was the same edition he had devoured as a boy in Africa.

It was a set of short stories depicting a harassed Mr. Parkhill— a night school teacher in New York in the 1930s, and his class of immigrants from Eastern Europe, seeking to improve their rudimentary English. His 'star' pupil, an ever-respectful student who contorted the speech and grammar of English into his own perverse logic, insisted on displaying his name as H*Y*M*A*N K*A*P*L*A*N in green stars between red letters outlined in blue. Kaplan's favourite Shakespearean character was Julius "Scissor". One Christmas, he presented Mr. Parkhill with a gift from all the pupils bearing the initials M.P. It took Mr. Parkhill a while before he realized that the 'M' stood for Mister.

Summers, for him as a teenager, were spent in Dar-es-Salaam, Tanzania, a refuge from his year-long schooling in England.

The 1970s were a hotbed of Socialism in the country governed by an ex-school teacher, Julius Nyerere. Ujamaa was introduced as a system of self-sustaining village cooperative for the economic development of Tanzania.

European governments loved Nyerere, donating billions to his cause and infesting the country with idealistic aid workers. They would come on contracts for three years, laden with enough books to last their sojourn. On their departure, the books were donated to Khan's Secondhand Books and Photocopying, established for a generation beside The Empire Cinema.

As a boy, he was their grateful beneficiary. Obtaining, for a trifle, the six volumes of *The Second World War* by Winston S. Churchill one day and Emile Zola the next. The brightly chalked cover of Hyman Kaplan captivated him—who, at the age of five, had been shipped off to England, with no knowledge of the language—to be brought up by an English working-class family who knew no other tongue.

Each episode of the book saw Kaplan set a torch to the English language, while all the time trying his hardest to master it, either through its inexplicable rules of spelling or the insane rules guiding its pronunciation. Each story saw Kaplan get the better of Mr. Parkhill as the perplexed teacher tried in vain to explain the arcane intricacies of the English language.

In one sentence that Kaplan wrote on the board for class scrutiny, his fellow learners found ten mistakes. Instead of leaving him embarrassed, Kaplan stood up and gazed at his masterpiece in awe that he had created such a puzzle for the class to solve.

As a five-year-old, beached upon an island of English kids in a classroom, he had neither the bravado nor the belief to question the teacher on the enigmatic syntax of sentences. Unlike Kaplan, he could not withstand the slings and arrows of his classmates. And so, he developed an admiration and affection for the character whose travails he shared. Besides, the stories were funny.

As his summer vacations drew to an end in Africa, he would meekly return the books he had read to Khan's—save for the dissertations of Hyman Kaplan. These volumes were kept in a hallowed glass-fronted bookcase until his return to Africa, or, as it happened, until his family fled the country, abandoning his precious memorabilia ...until they surfaced in Manhattan.

Like a glutton, he requisitioned all three books in the series, never daring to ask their price, handing over his VISA at arm's length.

It took him another ten minutes to reach the grandly festooned Bloomingdales, one of the jewels of New York shopping. As he entered, a group of several chunky men in expensive suits and a female dressed in crimson stood at the foot of the magnificent ornate stairs leading to the floors above, talking to each other while, at the same time, eyeing the customers.

He entered, a little bewildered, dressed as usual, like an over-weight jogger.

"Can we help you?" one of them asked. They looked and spoke like high-end security.

He would not be intimidated. "Yes, you can. Where are your Christmas Gund bears?"

"Sorry, we're sold out. We had over three thousand. You should have come sooner." One of the chunky suits answered with polished politeness.

"We just arrived from Canada. The bear was for a little girl in our family who's in hospital. We thought it would be the perfect gift for her." Crestfallen, he felt his voice tremble.

The man stood for a moment sizing him up. "Come with me." He beckoned and promptly led him to a side office and asked him to sit down.

He glanced around in trepidation. The airless, windowless chamber was dominated by a large walk-in safe.

The suit opened the safe and walked in, returning moments later with a chocolate brown Gund bear tucked neatly under his arm. A bright red and gold ribbon around the bear's neck authenticated its pedigree. The man handed it to him.

"Merry Christmas." The man smiled in amusement at his obvious discomfiture. He explained, "Our Christmas bears are most coveted. Each year we keep three locked away for someone just like you."

In typical American fashion, the man handed him his business card. It read 'Richard Mast, Senior Vice President,

Bloomingdales'.

Calgary wasn't immune to random acts of kindness either, although they were sometimes wrapped in fear and suspense.

Relying on its renowned oil industry, the city suffered intense cycles of boom and bust, which meant Christmases in Calgary were not universally full of cheer.

One year, when he lost his business and their home had been foreclosed, his family was living in a rented apartment and he had been unemployed for months. A few weeks before Christmas, he had found some work in Edmonton, a three hour drive north of Calgary.

On his way home, despite the snow blizzard outside, he was smiling. He was carrying $1,600 in cash—as the bank had closed his account—his family would have a fine Christmas after all.

As he stepped off the bus, a wind chill of -40C hit him full in the face. There was no local transport to be seen to take him home. In the distance he spotted a taxi. He ran to it and jumped in.

The taxi driver was sullen and in Arabic garb, his face a bush of hair. The passenger counted the fare in advance, so anxious was he to see his family. As the taxi crunched to a halt, he handed the driver some notes, telling him to keep the change.

His joy turned to weeping when he discovered that, in the rush to count his fare, he had left the sixteen hundred dollars in the cab. He had no clue which cab he had used and no clue who the driver was.

The next day, someone called home. "Did you lose some money in my cab? Can I come and drop it off to you?" The wallet had included his business card with the telephone number on it. All his money was restored to him, the taxi driver refusing any reward for his good deed.

Several days later, he received another call. It was from the local Sun newspaper. "We heard a Muslim taxi driver retrieved your cash. We would love to interview you for a story."

"No thanks," came his immediate and emphatic answer. For months he had been hiding from the taxman and a host of creditors—he refused to go bankrupt. He was damned if he was going to give himself away.

"Since the September 11 attack in New York, many Muslims, including your taxi driver, have been harassed. It would really help if we could publish a good news story about them—and particularly at Christmas." The reporter was persuasive, and after all, he did owe so much to the driver.

"As long as it's a small article and published somewhere in the back of the paper, I'll do it."

The reporter came to see him on a Thursday with a photographer at her side.

"Can you show me the cash?"

He did.

"Now, can you hold the notes like a fan in front of your face?"

Again, he did as he was told.

When it was over, he asked, "When will the story appear?"

"Most probably Sunday, depending on what other stories there are at the time."

On the proffered Sunday, he walked over to the nearest Tim Horton's to peek at the paper. Passing a Sun newspaper stand, he stopped and started to tremble. They had planted him on the front page, in colour, waving a wad of hundred-dollar bills. It took him minutes to find some coins and steady his fingers to drop them into the machine and obtain a copy. And there he was, his balloon face covering the whole front page with directions to the story within.

For weeks he received calls from his friends about the story. "Did you know..." Luckily for himself and his family, there were none from the government or his creditors.

Every year, be they Christian or Muslim, New Yorkers or Calgarians, Angels of Christmas came to visit him to remind him of the miracle of compassion.

In Bloomingdales, he bid farewell to the SVP and hurried through the store searching for his family before the store closed.

AUTHOR'S NOTE

Let It Be

My maternal grandmother, paternal aunt and English mother are my guardian angels.

In days of darkness, they come to me and whisper words of wisdom, "There will be an answer. Let it be."

ILLUSTRATOR'S NOTES

A day in New York visiting old haunts and meeting old "friends"—books and pastries!—tangled with visions of another distant Christmas, darkened by fear and financial hardship that ends in a great kindness.

*"...Where did **you** come from?"*

CHAPTER 5
NO WORD FOR IT

BOXING DAY ARRIVED and although New York or the rest of the United States didn't recognize it as a holiday, there were plenty of sales to binge on and window displays to drool over.

Fifth Avenue—the main shopping thoroughfare—began barely a block away from their hotel. In the twilight, Cartier beamed out at them with its iconic two-hundred-foot, bright red, lighted ribbon and eight-foot bow. According to the security guard posted outside its entrance, 95,000 LED lights were used to light them. The exterior of its oversized windows seemed to be encrusted with sparkling jewels, each a different colour. In reality, they were a myriad of individual, multi-coloured, multi-layered strings of LED lights. If 95,000 were used to light up the bow and ribbon, how many more were used to decorate the windows? Harry, the guard, had no answer.

In the blur of Christmas lights and rapid forays in and out of stores, they amassed their loot—a Michael Kors sky-blue leather shoulder bag for his wife and a dark leather jacket, as soft as down, for his younger son. He, in turn, capitulated to the shopping spree, purchasing a gorgeous Brioni silk shirt with purple and white stripes and a matching Isaiah seven-fold tie for himself from Jimmie, a thirty-year veteran server at Saks.

Wandering away from the crowd swept avenue, the four of them walked up Madison Avenue to gain a respite.

Squeezed in between a Rimowa luggage and a Mont Blanc pen store was the Minamoto Kitchoan, a Japanese confectioner. Its tiled floors and walls were of pale yellow with artwork reflecting thick black calligraphy within a bright mustard yellow checkered border. A black, highly lacquered wooden bench rested at the centre of the store—a token of Japanese minimalism.

Tiny open boxes of what looked like chocolates were displayed under glass counters. The tiny pieces were in pastel colours of lilac, powder blue, pale pink and beige. A petite Japanese server, immaculately coiffed and outfitted in a traditional, picturesque kimono came to them, carrying a mini black lacquered tray.

"Would you like to try a sample?"

He took one. It tasted like... nothing. "It tastes nothing like chocolate."

"No sir, these are Wagashi. They are plant-based, including mochi (rice cake), anko (azuki bean paste) and fruits," she smiled.

They returned to Fifth Avenue and his favourite store—Barnes and Noble.

Wherever he took his boys, he encouraged them to buy books and music from local artists. While Laura browsed through the interior decorating section—one of her perpetual hints that, after three decades, their home had to be renovated—he took his boys up to the second floor to the music department. While Chris chose Techno music which had driven his father crazy in the subway, he found a CD of a live concert performed by Joni Mitchell and James Taylor.

While waiting in line to be served, a display of the latest Platinum Edition of *The Official Scrabble Players Dictionary* caught his eye. He should buy a copy. This edition was so new that it hadn't arrived yet in Canada, although its additional 5,000 words were already being used in the tournaments he played in.

He had been playing Scrabble for over thirty years. It had begun, quite innocuously, in a dentist's waiting room in Calgary. Browsing through an issue of Reader's Digest, he came across an IQ test. Intrigued, as he had failed his high school exams and been constantly thought of as "having a few screws loose", he tested himself. He got 18 out of 20 right. According to the book, he was eligible to join MENSA, whose members have an IQ in the top 1% of the population. He took their supervised test and became a member.

He wasn't impressed. As a newcomer to Canada and in his early twenties, he wanted to join a group who would be full of active, get-up-and-go characters. Instead, for the most part, he found himself facing people who were extremely bright but couldn't communicate or inspire. They were in dead-end jobs and lonely.

MENSA's annual fee was $17. He tried to be diplomatic in his resignation. "I can't afford the fee this year." The contact at head office immediately responded with, "We'll pay for it."

Among the members, there was a fellow that reminded him of ET—he wore large silver-rimmed glasses that magnified his eyes several-fold just like the alien in the recent Steven Spielberg movie. His actual name was Bala and he professed his love for English and playing Scrabble. He may have loved the language, but he totally butchered it when speaking.

"I'm starting a Scrabble club at my home. Would you like to come?" Bala's eyes bored into him.

Having nothing else to do and never realizing he'd be stuck with him for the next thirty years, he accepted.

Bala had rounded up a group of eight. Unexpectedly, they were outgoing, full of banter, and half of them were females. This was the kind of group he had longed for. Most of them were young and English. All retained their quirky English humour. Thanks to Bala's superhuman soliciting, the group rapidly expanded to thirty. Instead of playing at each other's homes, a church basement had to be rented weekly.

Bala's zest overpowered all the originals except his MENSA colleague. The creative seven—employed in Advertising or similar disciplines—were replaced by hardened, no-nonsense Engineers and introspective Maths graduates.

The 'fun' wearied.

He was back in the same environment he had encountered when joining MENSA. His opponents learned all the mnemonics to plonk down 'Bingos'—when they used all their seven Scrabble tiles in one turn, earning a bonus 50 points and were virtually guaranteed to win the game. Memorizing all the words in the dictionary—without bothering to know their meaning or etymology—they challenged his words mercilessly, making him lose his turn and be even further behind. They had no patience for his AIRBAG until it was introduced in the next edition of *The Official Scrabble Dictionary.*

He refused to accept defeat and moved on. He was going to win on his terms using his love of English and not using cheat sheets and other paraphernalia.

During those dozens of years, decades of playing Scrabble, he found time to marry a non-Scrabble playing Filipina who bore him two boys who abhorred the game.

One summer, when his boys had become teenagers and his wife had taken them home to the Philippines to meet their grandparents, he once again became a Scrabble bachelor, taking his regular fix of the game every Thursday evening at the club.

On one such evening, his opponent turned out to be Bala.

"Why don't you come with us to Reno for the North American Scrabble Championship? It's 48 games over six days. We're renting a minivan and sharing rooms, and our hotel is giving us a huge discount. Come on, you've always refused. Now's your chance, while your family's away."

The master solicitor had found his mark.

As they continued their game, he looked across at Bala and assessed his own chances at Reno. By now, his Scrabble rating had been steadily declining. There were hundreds of players across the continent coming. With so many attendees, there would be at least four divisions. He'd be lucky if he got into the second or third, but at least he would have a chance to play and, in between, enjoy the desert sunshine.

A few weeks later, they arrived at Reno. Before the start of the tournament, Bala, whom he had studiously tried to avoid, found him and slapped him on the shoulder. "Congrats. You managed to sneak into the first division—you're the last seed. The bad news is they use Swiss pairing in the first round. You'll be playing the number one."

On tournament day, he entered the palatial casino ballroom, the largest in Reno. There were hundreds of tables, all row upon row regimented like an ancient Roman army phalanx beneath the over-bright, overheated, overpoweringly mighty chandelier. It was his first tournament away from Calgary and he had drawn the top player. He wanted to vomit.

He imagined the prelude to 'Gunfight at the OK Corral'. His opponent arrived with a swagger, offered a perfunctory handshake then completely ignored him while he laid out his paraphernalia—a tile tracking sheet, various felt pens and biro—and then reset the time clock.

He looked at his own apparatus—one half-chewed pen—hoping it wouldn't smudge or run out of ink. He willed his hands to stop shaking.

They drew for first. The champion drew an F. He drew an E. The player closer to the beginning of the alphabet went first.

He drew his seven tiles. No vowels. Now what? Convention dictated a player never exchange all their letters. Keep at least two. He changed them all, forfeiting his turn and any advantage he might have had going first against his opponent.

The champ glared at him quizzically and played a 36 pointer.

He reviewed his new rack: AUUIIIE. There was nowhere on the board to play more than two letters. The maximum he'd score was 6. He changed all his tiles again.

The number one player continued his annihilation, playing Joes for 40 points. Thankfully, with such an open board, he still hadn't found a Bingo.

For the third time, he reviewed his new rack of tiles. Glory be! He had a blank tile that he could use as any letter he wished. And, he had a Bingo AND he had a spot for it, provided his opponent didn't block it. He didn't.

A 92-point play! Now he was only 20 points behind.

Adrenalin rushed through his body. His tiles were improving— he had a chance of winning. If he could score at least 30 points in the next two turns and prevent his opponent from scoring a Bingo.

Word-by-word, he advanced on the champ.

His final turn—22 points behind. He had five tiles left: MYAF and O. He found it! And a spot to play it. FOAMY for 31 points.

The champion challenged.

Convention dictates that on a challenge, both parties walk to the Word Judge to determine whether the word challenged is good or not. This is to avoid any tampering.

The champion refused to budge from his seat, making him walk all the way down the line of tables alone, the other players all turning to look at him.

Of course, the word was good—even a novice knew it. The champion had deliberately insulted him in retaliation for his loss.

The champion could barely sign the official tally slip acknowledging his loss. His hands were clenched into fists.

"Where are you from?" he spat out in barely recognizable American-English.

"From Calgary."

"And where's that?"

He told him and, in return asked, "And where are you from?"

"New York!"

"Where's that?"

The champion stood up, his hands still clenched. For a moment, he looked as if he was going to throw a punch. Instead, he turned abruptly leaving the table and all his accoutrements behind.

At Barnes and Noble, as he perused the dictionary for new words, Chris nudged him in the ribs with disgust. "Not Scrabble again?"

How could he explain to the godless his love affair with this game? He had no word for it.

AUTHOR'S NOTES

Across the Universe

Words are flowing out like endless rain into a paper cup

They slither wildly as they slip away across the universe

*Pools of sorrow, waves of joy are drifting through
my opened mind*

Possessing and caressing me

Through Chaos came our world

Through Scrabble my stories

ILLUSTRATOR'S NOTES

*In the temple of a beloved game confronted by an
opponent who sees you as an upstart or 'lesser than',
a dragon with an oversized ego surges out of the dark
corners demanding to know who this interloper is!*

"...what had been lost in the taking?"

CHAPTER 6

NO ADOBO TONIGHT

WOULD THIS BLIZZARD ever end? He glared out of the hotel window at the Manhattan skyline seemingly close enough to touch, the wind blowing the snow in frantic circles. While he bemoaned the weather, Laura sat on the couch glued to her iPad chuckling.

"They're on the way, running late because of the weather," she said. "Look at this. Here's their latest photo." He peered over her shoulder at her screen.

"Alma looks so much older. Lani's put on some weight." For the umpteenth time she reminded him that they were all at high school together, graduating in '75 and hadn't seen each other since Lani and Laura left the Philippines.

"Lani went back home last year to marry her childhood sweetheart, Jerry. He was also in our batch." She retrieved their grad photo. "She trained as a nurse and emigrated to New Jersey. She and Jerry married soon after. His first wife died of cancer two years ago. He and Lani reconnected through Facebook," She continued. "Alma remained in Bacolod and married Rico, another of our batch. They both emigrated to New Jersey a few months ago. Their son sponsored them. I think they're retired."

Many years ago, when iPads first came out, he gave her one as a surprise birthday present. In marrying Laura, he discovered you could take the girl out of the Philippines, but you couldn't take the Philippines out of the girl. Each night when he got home, she greeted him with a radiant smile, rushing to show him her iPad.

"Hon, hon, guess what?" She thrust the screen in his face. "I found Victor, an old friend, on Facebook. He's working as a mechanic in Doha, Qatar. Look, he's sent me a photo." Over the subsequent months, she traced Freddy in Cyprus and Nicole Kelly in Dubai. The list became endless as she added cousins and nephews and nieces.

Every summer, whenever husband and wife travelled, Laura, through her iPad, found one of her Filipina friends to meet for lunch or supper. To each rendezvous she carted her husband along to share in her celebratory connection to home.

Her friends welcomed him like family. Each Filipino word would be followed by an English one to accommodate him.

Having been brought up since the age of five by a conservative English family who always conducted themselves with typical English reserve, he was overwhelmed by the Filipinas' natural warmth and generosity of spirit. Despite the great divide in culture and speech, he found their innocence and fierce devotion to their family, friends and homeland touching, even though many of them hadn't returned to the Philippines in decades, sending all their spare income to those back home. Despite the differences, this was the one common bond that drew him ever closer to them.

Each Christmas, they turned up at the same Sari-Sari (grocery) store at the end of East Bay Street in Nassau, surrounded by off-duty Filipino sailors. They'd sit at tables tucked away in a corner while a grandmother prepared food for them. There, Laura caught up with old friends who were nannies to multi-millionaires seeking tax shelter in the Bahamas. In summer, they negotiated narrow, ancient cobbled alleys in Nicosia, Cyprus to reach a shack on its last legs to slurp down Halo-Halo—a colourful milk and ice-cream dessert full of nuts, beans and fruits—with friends she hadn't seen in decades.

While he loved their desserts—hundreds ranging from coconut cakes to bananas wrapped in thin crispy pastry, coated in streaks of caramel—he found their main courses bland. But one dish he always ordered was Adobo—chicken pieces in thick brown sauce cooked in black peppers.

He was never sure whom he would meet at these get-togethers. Laura, reserved and demure in Canada, lit up among a circle of friends far greater in diversity and numbers than his own. One could be a doctor, another a nanny. Many were nurses. But there was a common thread. Due to family pressures, all had left home to support their large families. These were the eldest kids—the first to leave—now all in their fifties like Laura.

Laura had left home in 1984 at the age of twenty-five, with two university degrees and a well-paid, respected position in a publishing house. Although her salary was ample for her own needs, it was inadequate to support the rest of her family. So, she left, never having travelled out of her town except once, to the nearby island of Cebu. Upon graduation, her school offered a yearbook to purchase or the trip. She couldn't afford both so opted to take the opportunity to travel.

Bacolod was her hometown whose mainstay was the harvesting of sugarcane. Once the market slumped, no one in her family could find work and half her siblings were still in school. To her, there was no choice but to work abroad. Once she emigrated, her life fell into a tailspin. A university graduate with two degrees, a middle-class upbringing and well-paid job, she found herself employed as a nanny in Singapore, working six days a week with a broom cupboard for a bedroom. She cried when she remembered the brand-new bed she had recently bought in Bacolod.

Her friends shared similar tales of being abruptly dragged out of a secure, comforting environment and into the depths of uncertainty and subservience in an alien one.

There was a knock at the door. Her friends had arrived.

It was as though a tornado had blown in. There was a gust of laughter and voices, hugs and handshakes as they introduced themselves to him, each not knowing what to expect from the other.

As they entered, his boys tried to leave. They were joining friends from Calgary who'd shown up in New York for the day. Their mum would not allow them to leave before presenting them to her friends.

His eyes wandered from his six-foot-three kids bending down to hug the Filipinos—all five-foot-four like Laura and himself. His boys had been born in Canada, spoke English perfectly and had attended private schools all their lives. They, along with their friends, were off to see The Book of Mormon. Then glancing again at the Filipinos, he could imagine them later, huddled in a Sari-Sari store slurping Halo-Halo. It was like the Western world politely tolerated but never quite accepted these immigrants as one of their privileged own.

He caught Laura's attention. "Hon, the weather's really bad. I can't find a Sari-Sari close by. The only reasonably priced restaurant around here is Bistro Chez Jacques. Would that be alright? It's only a block away." He turned to their guests for approval.

"Great idea. We haven't been to a bistro in months," Lani confirmed. She took Jerry out to restaurants regularly. They pulled on their snow jackets and fur boots ready to go. Both seemed to have become natives of the country.

Alma stared out the window, dumbstruck by the Manhattan skyline. It was her first trip to New York. Her husband waited for everyone to approve the restaurant before he nodded. Both he and Alma seemed relieved they wouldn't have to walk far to the Bistro—they were still wearing shoes and coats fit for fall.

As they emerged from their hotel, the girls walked hand-in-hand in front of them. He had witnessed this in Asia and in the Gulf states where Filipinas would do the same.

It was too bloody cold to start a conversation. They protected themselves as best as they could against the biting wind and gusting snow outside, almost jog-trotting to their destination.

Set on the corner of Fifth Avenue and 59th Street, the Bistro

Chez Jacques had a revolving door as its entrance The walls were white and framed in glossy black moldings. Brilliantly coloured Toulouse-Lautrec posters hung haphazardly upon the walls. Yet, to him the Bistro had no atmosphere, no joie de vivre—a canteen that filled for a couple of hours with patrons who were always in transit.

Tonight, it was packed with theatre goers. The Maitre d' found a corner spot for them away from the main thoroughfare. He handed them menus and a wine list before leaving. " Your waiter will be with you shortly. Are you in a hurry to get to your show?"

"No." He said, shaking his head.

The menu was tall, dark and narrow in embossed leather with gold braid running down its fold. He reviewed it and sighed with relief. It was eclectic enough for all of them. Besides pâtés and Coquilles Saint-Jacques, their signature dish, there were also american burgers with kaiser buns encrusted with poppy seeds and real fries–the way only the French can make them. There was also chicken and fish. All the menu lacked was Filipino food.

He smiled to himself. There would be no Adobo tonight.

Reluctantly, having eyed the burger and fries covetously, he ordered some hummus, toasted pita chips and Greek salad without feta cheese to combat his burgeoning weight. The waiter appeared wearing all black including his beret. A large sparkling white apron hung down his front. Over one shoulder lay a crisply folded white linen napkin. From a side pocket he took out a miniscule note pad and retrieved a pencil resting behind his ear.

Once their orders were taken, Laura and her friends returned to their animated conversation. Again, her husband was forgotten.

"I saw Victor last summer."

"Oh, yes? Whatever happened to his wife?"

"Marilou found work in Frankfurt and married a banker."

And on it went.

All five were so engrossed in their reminiscences he didn't have the heart to intervene or contribute nor impinge on their evident contentment.

They had been married for twenty-five years. Not a month passed without a crisis call from the Philippines. Half the time she wouldn't even tell him. He was an early riser, she a late one. Sometimes he would wake up and go downstairs. Laura would be on the phone, anxiety in her voice. He would quietly slip away to save her any embarrassment. Occasionally, he would surreptitiously glance at her and notice the worry on her face. It seemed the only time that burden lifted was when she was among her fellow exiles.

Despite obtaining two university degrees, Laura hated studying and only did the minimum required to pass. She skipped school in the afternoons to play basketball with Alma. Nonetheless, she still managed to keep up with the likes of Lani, a school-teacher's daughter. It was Lani who graduated from nursing school cum laude, then emigrated independently to the US. She was now a head nurse at her hospital. It was the combination of sports and academics that made Laura so popular among her peers and resulted in the wide range of friends she made.

On completing her contract in Singapore, Laura found another job as a nanny in Calgary. It was all she could find despite her qualifications. As her Filipina friends in Singapore returned home, she felt it her duty to persevere. Her family depended on her financial support.

He met Laura in Calgary, working as a bookkeeper. By then, she had completed her two-year stint as a nanny, gained landed immigrant status and was now able to work where she wished. She chose her former profession of accounting. He was an accountant himself, working for the same company.

At first, he had found her reserved and introverted. Gradually, she opened up as she gained more and more trust in him. But she kept her conversation with others to the barest minimum. Eventually, the penny dropped. He began to understand her reticence to speak to others.

Although born to East Indians, he had grown up in England. In Canada, his natural English accent gave him a sense of superiority.

Only now, in observing his wife among her own peers talking so confidently in her native tongue of Tagalog, did he realize how difficult it would be living in Canada, speaking in faltering English and being judged by your inability to speak clearly. To many of these immigrants, including Laura who was a perfectionist, their shame stilled their tongues.

The main course ended and as they waited for their coffee and creme brulee, Laura discretely pulled out two small paper bags from under the table and presented them to Lani and Alma.

"Wow!" Lani said. "Suites in Essex House overlooking Central Park. Perfumes for us from Bloomingdales. You guys must be doing reeaally well." Alma opened her presents, smelled the perfume, and put it back in the box.

In Calgary, when Laura first invited him to her apartment, he had laughed and laughed. Both had been living in Calgary for years. Her apartment was spick and span, and there was the barest of furniture and little of personal commitment to staying. He also had the barest of furniture in a one room bachelor suite. Both their mantras were identical. "I'm saving my money to go home and start a business."

Where did he consider his home to be? In Africa, a place he had left as a child? Did he have anyone there he knew? No.

At least she did.

The abandonment of their former home and community propelled them to continuously strive to retrieve what they had lost, no matter how ephemeral that life had been compared to their years in exile. Retrieval came in the form of rare visits home supplemented by the slurping of Halo-Halo in a rundown shack in some anonymous back street of a bustling metropolis.

Many were now comfortably settled in their country of exile. Then there were the Almas and Ricos of the world, self-expelled from their homeland to join their children abroad after decades of separation. What would they have in common now? How could parents, in the first place, allow their naive and innocent children to leave home to support a family they had borne? With no knowledge or preparation of the perils and hardship they were to face? And to have their children arrive abroad as menials with no rights or respect and equality stripped from them in the process—be they a nanny in Canada or a construction worker in Qatar.

What happiness could children afford to give their parents while tearing them away from their homeland?

His East Indian Muslim mother had divorced his father shortly before he was parcelled off to England. Years after settling in Canada, he sponsored both his parents. While his mother willingly moved to Calgary, his father insisted in joining his bosom buddies in Toronto. For thirty years, he had worked in Africa in a large airline office supervising a dozen staff. He had a palatial home to live in. His friends in Canada found him work manufacturing metal cabinets. Earning minimum wage and facing two hours travelling a day, he found himself sharing a basement with three of his friends in the same predicament.

Once, he had visited his father in Toronto and vowed never again. He could not bear to see the life his father now led compared to the halcyon days of his childhood when he visited Africa and watched his father play cricket twice a week with the Baby Tuskers—seeming to have all the time in the world to enjoy himself. His father never complained as he admonished him. "Times change my son."

At Bistro Chez Jacques, he heard Laura ask Lani the perennial question, "Have you been back home recently?"

"I was there in August. Mum was sick. There was no one else to look after her. My dad died a few years ago."

He thought of his immediate family and what they had experienced together. Somehow, despite the cyclical economic oil slumps in Calgary, he had rescued his wife from the chronic pressure of earning for herself and her family in the Philippines. His two boys were well-educated Canadians. And his home in Africa a family myth

Within that progress of survival rolling into financial security and on to wealth, what had been lost in the taking? Did his kids appreciate what they had? A place of belonging and privilege? Or

71

would they too be soon sitting down with their affluent friends discussing the merits of Tesla cars and international destinations at dinner, while being served by the nameless and forgotten, be they African or Filipino?

AUTHOR'S NOTE

You Can't Take the Philippines Out of The Girl

Thirty years since she's left the country and still each day my wife talks of her home, her friends and the food she misses.

I sigh as each day I too revert to the past in my writing.

The past that snares and entwines us all.

ILLUSTRATOR'S NOTE

A little magic realism on a cold snowy New York night, illustrating the idea of being 'blown around the world' by design, fate or circumstance and what, weighed in the balance, will be the cost of that—even if you're successful—for your children.

"Do you want to be our controller?"

CHAPTER 7
FOAMING TEA

"**POPS, CAN WE** go eat? I'm hungry," Chris asked. The whole family had been traipsing the sky-scrapered streets of New York, passing one modern building after another, waging their own war against the scalding wind chapping their faces. He glanced at his watch. Already 2 p.m. They had left their hotel in Upper Manhattan shortly after nine that morning.

Turning a corner, it appeared they had walked through a time warp, stepping back fifty years. There were no buildings taller than two storeys. Garbage piled up the corners. Power cables swung on wooden poles along the street. The poles seemed to sway in the wind, sometimes coming to rest at an angle. Along the street stood row-upon-row of shops selling everything from black lacquered chopsticks to earthen rice pots interrupted only by ra dom rinky-dink one-room restaurants. Ancient greying signs, all in Chinese, hung precariously over entrances, complementing the ubiquitous metallic-grey sky. This was Chinatown.

"Ooh! Let's go in there." Again, from Chris. His father had no time to consult his guidebook to find an approved restaurant.

The Chinese Fortune restaurant, its name emblazoned in glaring gold and red English, jumped out at them in all its glory.

An aroma of strong vinegar and burnt garlic hit him as he entered the restaurant which was no bigger than a closet. Four round tables, nine feet in diameter, vied for every inch of space available. Each table sprouted double the chairs necessary. A waiter in a stained, yellowing white apron ushered his family of four to a table half occupied by other diners. It was like being in China, where there was rarely the luxury of individual tables for each set of customers. A chef's hole linked the smoky, steaming hot kitchen to its patrons.

He could hardly lodge himself into his seat without nudging his neighbour. Having succeeded in depositing themselves in adjoining seats, Laura, and the boys couldn't extricate themselves to leave. The other diners, all aggressively Chinese in their speech and manner, sat elbow-to-elbow eyeing the four strangers. The constant clatter of plates, as though they were being flung to the floor, competed with the loud cacophony of loud voices between the waiter, continuously going outdoors to smoke, and his bad-tempered customers.

The waiter dumped a teapot and four tiny china cups in front of them, then stood waiting for their order. There were no menus, only Chinese characters written on a notice board balancing precariously from a nail. The waiter refused to speak

English. Confusion reigned between husband and wife. All they could understand of the menu was the price of each dish—all under $10. The weather squelched any enthusiasm to leave and try elsewhere. Laura asked him to choose. It was like picking lottery numbers. He hoped he had chosen a winning combination. He dreaded Chris's reaction to his choices. Another fine mess you got us into.

The Monster, Chris, was at a stage in life where everything his father did was scrutinized and criticized to the bone. Chris may have chosen the restaurant, but it would be forgotten under a barrage of complaints if the food wasn't just right. Unfortunately for his father, most times the criticism proved too right, leaving his father resentful and belligerent towards his son.

As Laura poured out tea for them, he stared at the teapot and cups. They were identical to the ones at the Golden Inn, the first Chinese restaurant he ever ate at, snuggled in a corner at the bottom of Centre Street Bridge in Calgary, Canada. He was taken there as a guest of Joe—his boss—very late one night because it stayed open until 4 a.m. and because it was the only restaurant in Chinatown that served foaming tea. Golden Inn became his favourite restaurant and its waiters his steadfast friends in the decades to come.

In the early eighties, Chinese restaurants had no liquor licence. To certain esteemed patrons, the Inn served 'foaming tea' when requested. As he gulped down spicy squid, Golden Inn's signature dish, he noticed his boss downing his tea one cup after another in quick succession. He couldn't understand Joe's relish for tea until his boss poured some out for him. Expecting steaming tea, his tongue met cold liquid and realized it was beer.

Joe, a bachelor with no siblings and parents who had died in a car crash when he was ten, had abandoned school at fifteen to work at a building site. Within a few years, he had befriended a gypsy, borrowed $25,000 in cash from him and purchased a rundown 16-suite apartment building. The oil boom was at its height. By the time they met over spicy squid, Joe owned 300 rental homes and dozens of apartment buildings. He badly needed a professional accountant to keep him straight.

While Joe amassed a fortune, his dinner companion had recently emigrated from England as a chartered accountant and was in his second year at Collins Barrow. He had been assigned to prepare Joe's annual corporate financial statements and tax returns.

Each day as he entered the client's office, he was greeted by a tall, slightly overweight man, propped up against the filing cabinet behind the receptionist, a toothpick stuck in his mouth. They were never introduced. The man wasn't particularly well-dressed. The accountant presumed he was the office errand boy.

It was a daunting and unusual challenge for the accountant. There were over eighty joint ventures to reconcile. Apart from bank statements, there were no accounting records. Everything for the business with over a hundred million dollars in real estate was kept in Joe's head. Nora was his bookkeeper, but never allowed the time to do any accounting. She spent her working life catering to Joe's every whim and fancy, picking up and dropping off his laundry, sorting out daily problems with the property managers, including emergencies, maintenance, and vetting invoices. All the while also being the office receptionist.

The office was part of a large apartment tower. Joe had converted three penthouse suites into one unit for himself. He placed Homer, a sixty-year-old drinking buddy of his, as the building manager. Homer knew nothing about property management and didn't seem to care. He drove Nora crazy.

Normally, the accountant from Collins Barrow was given at least two assistants and several months to complete his work. At their last meeting, John Collins, the senior partner, announced, "We're short of staff. We have no one to help you. Can you get Nora to assist? By the way, you've got a month to get the job done. Joe's made a huge profit this year and we need to file his taxes on time."

Pulling information together was a nightmare. Joe shunned paperwork of any sort and kept all his deals between himself and his lawyer. He knew the amount of each mortgage payment. At the very last minute, he would summon Nora into his office to write out the cheques, then ask her to hand-deliver them to the banks. Being new to the account, all his knowledge of Joe came from Nora or from the overheard conversations she would have with him.

Somehow, with the help of Nora and working seven days a week, he completed his assignment on time.

On his last day, Nora asked him to accompany her. She led him down a corridor to a large office with the blinds down and lights off, save for a desk lamp. On the wall stood a limited-edition print splashed in vibrant colours by Leroy Neiman, depicting a horse race. A three-foot square of two-dollar bills hung on one wall, framed, and glassed. A Velcro dartboard with giant darts thrust into it clung to the wall farther down. An obligatory Calgary Stampede bronze figure of a horse bucking a cowboy stood on a dark wooden pedestal.

Through the gloom, he discerned a humungous table, solid as a mountain. Upon it lay documents in piled disorder, dozens of discarded envelopes of all sizes and colours, tattooed with scrawls and scribbles. Sitting behind the table, his head swallowed in his hands, sat the errand boy.

It was Joe. He tried to open his eyes but gave up halfway. In a voice barely audible, he asked, "Do you want to be our controller?"

At the Chinese Fortune, their food arrived. A plate of tripe and bok choy in garlic sauce which Laura devoured. The boys gobbled up sizzling rice with all kinds of meats and vegetables, while he contently savoured sweet eggplant stuffed with large shrimp.

No sooner had the food been demolished, Chris started to lay into his brother.

"Why can't we go back to the hotel and play Civilization?" demanded Chris.

"Because I want to walk over to Union Square to collect a book from Barnes and Noble," came the irritated reply from Alex, the Poodle. Surprising, as Alex generally went with the flow, rarely insisting on his way. Neither asked their parents what they wanted to do.

Monster? Poodle? Why had their father given them such nicknames bordering on the derogatory? Sure, Chris was a monster and Alex sported a ridiculous hairstyle. There was an ambivalence towards his boys that the father could never reconcile.

Alex was a clone of his mother. Apart from his hair, he never caused a problem. He sailed through life pleasing everyone, yet all the same, getting his every wish without anyone noticing—except his father. Alex had been born in a time of financial security with untold optimism for what the future held, buoyed by countless attentive family friends.

Then, another major recession hit Calgary in 1994, a year after he was born and nine months before his brother. The family's custom-built mansion on a hill with its panoramic view of the city and mountains was foreclosed as each of his father's businesses closed and their personal belongings auctioned off.

He couldn't remember when he had given Chris the nickname Monster, probably before he was born. The fear and stress his mother felt during her pregnancy was all bottled up within her. But her anger was released through Chris. He charged out of the womb bellicose and highly colicky. The merest sound, say someone walking down the corridor of their hospital ward, left him bellowing with all his might. Chris was born into a decade of turmoil, despondency, and total withdrawal from their circle of friends. They had no family in Calgary.

While Alex smiled at everyone, Chris bared his teeth at one and all. His father had once been proud of being the only father at his school to drop off and collect his sons with not a day missed. By the time Grade 12 arrived, Chris was full of woe and tribulation. He waged war on his teachers daily to a point where his parents were never sure what they would face when retrieving him from school. His father gave up the struggle and refused to drive him.

The truth was, Chris was just like his father. The father had failed his exams at school—too busy fighting and annoying everyone around him. Father and son both questioned everything, always searching for answers to questions they couldn't formulate. The father saw the weaknesses in himself reflected in his son, flaws that he would never admit to but was forced to endure in his son.

The father's ambivalence towards their elder son was also caked in resentment. Halfway through Grade 12, Alex stated quite matter-of-factly, he would win the student of the year award. And he did. It wasn't just grades that were considered. It included having a 100% attendance record and never being late for school. It included good sportsmanship, social participation and school spirit. His father failed his high school and was always told he was a failure.

There was a love-hate relationship between the brothers. Chris strove for his brother's attention and affection. When he didn't get the desired result, he turned to bickering with and belittling his elder brother.

A different form of bickering took place in Calgary between Nora and Homer. Partly to assert power, partly a contest for Joe's affection. Nora loved Joe, but finding he showed more interest in Homer than in her, she took her resentment out on the poor property manager. Besides, in Joe's absence, she was regarded as the only authority. It galled her that she could neither intimidate nor control Homer.

It wasn't only Nora and Homer that Joe encouraged to butt heads. He did it to everyone. Nobody seemed to see it or acknowledge it. Joe had the charm of an Irish leprechaun, even though he was Jewish. Outwardly, he was loved by all—never was a bad word spoken against him. But it didn't take long for his accountant to figure his boss out. To Joe, it was a matter of maintaining control, whether it was by setting one employee against another or grudgingly imparting the barest information to his accountant. Having something put down on paper appalled him.

"Pops, look over there." Chris was pointing at four elderly Chinese seated around a fold-up card table in the corner. They were playing Mahjong. "Can we join them?"

Working from home, his father spent evenings, weekends and holidays teaching and playing all kinds of board games with his sons, including Mahjong. He and Alex enjoyed games for the sake of playing, Chris for the sake of winning. Chris learned strategy swiftly and never relinquished an inch to his opponent. His father taught him chess and Chris became school champion year-after-year, inevitably beating his brother in the finals. Yet, come summer, his parents waited anxiously, ever expecting him to fail and have to repeat a grade.

He had been taught to play Backgammon by Joe and in turn taught and played it with Chris—until he lost so much money that he gave up.

Each office day around 10.30 a.m. Joe, surrounded by half a dozen of his cronies, would be pouring out drams of Glenfiddich whisky in his office and playing Backgammon. His accountant, always left in the dark as to the deals Joe had made or was about to make, began to realize the importance of being allowed into these sessions where gossip abounded, and news was exchanged about the goings-on in Calgary's real estate market. It was there that Joe let his guard down.

One weekend, out of the blue, Joe invited him to his vacation home beside Chestermere Lake on the outskirts of town. There he was taught to play Backgammon by Joe and his buddies.

That weekend lost him a thousand dollars but returned him a fortune in intelligence and contacts. Through rheumy eyes and smoke-induced headaches, he attained a level good enough to challenge Joe at his own game. From then on, he was summoned daily to the 10.30 a.m. sessions with Joe and his cronies.

The accountant could now keep abreast of whatever was going on with Joe. He was also introduced to many of Joe's business partners on an intimate basis. Some had tax problems, others operational issues. Joe allowed him consult to them, provided his own work was done on time.

It would have taken Joe several lifetimes to spend the money he had. And he had no one to leave it to.

All his buddies would be away over winter and travelling the weekends. Joe never budged from home.

"Joe, get away from the cold. Come to Palm Springs with us over Christmas." They would plead.

"Joe, come to Vegas for the Backgammon tournament at the Sands." He was tempted but always changed his mind at the last minute.

The invitations were endless. His popularity never waned.

Joe rarely strayed from the orbit of his apartment and office which were interlinked physically and seemed to have a hold over him psychologically. Somehow, he feared the collapse of his empire if he left it unattended for even a day.

Greed was Joe's downfall.

The year his accountant joined him, was successful for Joe. The mortgages on his 300 houses had been paid up and most of his apartment buildings too. Joe took a fraction of the profits for himself and spread the rest on the Monopoly board that Calgary had become under the auspices of a gigantic oil boom.

"Joe, why don't you partner with me?" one of his best friends asked him. "I just built and sold an office tower off Blackfoot Trail and made a bundle. You have the whole block off 14th Avenue in single homes. Roll in your properties at market value—that's at least four times what you paid for them. I have my construction company. I'll match your contribution with the cost of my staff, building permits and material to build condos. We'll split the profits."

An offer too good to refuse.

Joe never liked being second best to any of his friends. The trouble was his friend had fifty on his payroll with no assets to match. Cash flow came in only on the sale of a property and the payment of bills was a monthly headache. Meanwhile, Joe had little debt and far too much cash flow. He had an office staff of six, all, except the accountant, on minimum wage and chosen for being uneducated and easily controlled.

Before Joe had completed the first joint venture, a second came along and then a third until he had more than twenty multi-million-dollar projects on the go and partners with no assets and ever consuming overheads. The risks involved made Joe's accountant cringe. But his boss paid no heed to his remonstrations. Times were booming and opportunity rife. The banks loved Joe, giving him credit lines of $12,000,000 that he could draw on without recourse to anyone.

The slump arrived.

Interest rates rocketed to over 20% per annum. Homes were sold for a dollar as their owners fled the province—having lost their jobs they couldn't make their mortgage payments. One by one, Joe's partners bit the dust. As each declared bankruptcy, Joe took on their burden, furiously writing cheques from his lines of credit until nothing was left of the $12,000,000.

It was a bright, sunny but bone-chilling winter morning. The accountant headed to work early to complete a statement. On entering, he noticed the lights were on in Joe's office. The cleaners must have forgotten to switch them off. As he stepped closer, he heard a voice, "Joe, the banks have called in a receiver." It was Dave, Joe's cousin and only relative. "They tried to call you last night, but you were out. The receiver's coming in first thing this morning." Like a pack of jackals, the banks had turned on him.

Joe's accountant, along with the rest of the staff were fired on the spot. Joe disappeared. "He's out of town and can't be reached," was all they could get out of Dave.

As the weeks passed, his accountant heard Joe had made a lucrative deal with the banks. He would stay on and help the banks sell all their properties in return for a hefty consulting fee.

Meanwhile, Joe mustered all his friends who still had money and persuaded them to buy his properties at fire-sale prices. He would share in the profits when the properties were resold. His friends held and operated the now-affordable properties, making a killing a few years later when the economy rebounded. Eventually, Joe was installed as president and worth millions again.

His former accountant remained in Calgary, weathered the economic storm and made a comeback, though not as spectacularly as his ex-boss.

In all that time, Joe kept completely away from his former accountant, neither offering him condolences nor his job back. Joe had hired a totally new set of staff.

Several years rolled by.

One Friday afternoon, the accountant was picking up his wife from work in downtown Calgary, close to Joe's new office. As they drove down 4th Avenue, a dark blue Chrysler New Yorker hurtled past then abruptly cut in front of them and stopped, forcing the accountant to slam on his brakes and screech to a halt.

The driver of the New Yorker got out and approached him. It was Joe. "Thank you for all you did for me." He turned back immediately, got into his car, and drove off before either husband or wife could react.

"Who was that? How did he know it was you?" asked Laura, still quivering.

"A guy I used to work for. He must have recognized my licence plate KASSARE—my dad's nickname." He stopped to catch his breath.

Next day, he received a phone call from Dave. "Joe's dead. He was going blind and had to hand in his New Yorker last night. Anna, his cleaner found him this morning. He was in the Jacuzzi with an empty bottle of Glenfiddich beside him. He'd been dead all night. Funny, his doctor had told him not to drink in the Jacuzzi as he had a weak heart." To the accountant, it said Joe was still petrified of losing his grip over everyone around him. He couldn't bear the thought of depending on those very people he had abused.

In the restaurant, Chris leapt out of his chair followed in quick succession by his brother. Their father had no choice but to dash after them to stop them from disturbing the Chinese Mahjong players.

As he rose from the table, his wife poured out some tea. She tugged his sleeve beckoning him to join her. Forced to sit down, he watched with trepidation as the boys were welcomed to the game.

AUTHOR'S NOTE

Letting Go

The turning point in my career came when I was let into my boss's morning Backgammon sessions.

Anxiously, I watched my boys drift away into the arms of strangers by way of Mahjong.

ILLUSTRATOR'S NOTE

A family dinner in a hole-in-the-wall Chinese diner in New York brings back memories of a different Chinese diner in Calgary and a boss whose corrosive idea of control was to pit employees against each other —who will win the "match" to earn his favour!

"He had no choice but to fight."

CHAPTER 8

JUDGEMENT DAY

THE WEATHER GODS had taken a day off. As mother and father looked onto Central Park from their boys' large window, they saw the obligatory winter mix of snow-laden grey sky and face-slapping ocean wind had abated. Trees no longer swayed wildly as though in a ballet. Sunshine swathed the park from the doorstep of their hotel far into Harlem. It was noon and time to explore.

They had been in New York since before Christmas Day. Now, a week later, the family had still not visited the Park. The atrocious weather had held them captive in thick layered clothing and fur-lined hoods. Their heads bowed to shelter their wind-chapped faces only gave them peripheral views of the city along with the minutiae of the black-iced pavement immediately in front of them.

Departing the JW Marriot Essex House, they walked in balmy sunshine almost tropical in its feel. No head coverings. Everyone was smiling for the first time since they arrived. Above the fuel-laden stink of heavy traffic, the aroma of roasted chestnuts overwhelmed his senses. A street vendor stationed beside his trolley, ladled chestnuts out of a brazier and emptied them into paper bags, steam rising. He bought two bagsful to share.

They crossed the busy street, avoided the line of horse-drawn carriages offering rides, and entered Central Park.

The size and variety of monuments in Manhattan baffled him. Either they were too large or too small. None ever seemed to be just right. Skyscrapers were overwhelming, the Statue of Liberty and Wall Street too small compared to their reputation. In England, where he had grown up, statuary and monuments celebrated heroes and statesmen, or iconic victories—such as Lord Nelson in Trafalgar Square, London. Here in New York, one never knew what to expect.

He guided his family across the cast-iron Bow Bridge, toured Central Park Lake, then turned right to inspect the magnificent, early twentieth century architecture on upper 5th Avenue—the Museum Mile.

"Hon, look at these buildings," he turned to Laura. She'd disappeared. So had the boys. In a panic, he reversed his direction in pursuit of them. Where the hell were they?

He found them standing in front of an eleven-foot-high bronze statue of Alice in Wonderland. A visiting Japanese tourist had been persuaded to take a photo of them. He in turn, with no real grasp of English was urging them to smile and raise their fingers in a peace salute.

Who but Americans would raise an eleven-foot statue to Alice? The other day, taking a break from grocery shopping, he had visited Strawberry Fields on his own. Another monument in the Park, this one was to celebrate John Lennon. No statue for him, only a nine-foot diameter round mosaic cut into a footpath with the word Imagine at its centre.

Alice stood behind a large bronze mushroom, the Mad Hatter and White Rabbit on either side of her. The smiling Cheshire Cat sat upon her shoulder. The statues looked as though some parts had been over-polished and the sun reflected brightly off them. He wondered why and found his answer a minute later; kids were clambering all over them leaving well-worn patches.

Something was missing. Where was the Queen of Hearts with her "Off with his head!" as the solution to the slightest annoyance?

As a child he had come across such a woman in his East Indian mother. No matter how much she cared for him, his most common memory was her outbursts of "My way or no way". With her, it wasn't "Off with his head!" but still the peremptory "Go to your room".

That attitude had never worked to better him, except once when it saved him from dishonour and perdition.

A decade ago, back in Canada...

According to the Canada Revenue Agency (CRA) he was as guilty as sin. They sequestered his bank statements, interviewed his clients and accused him of amassing undeclared income over the last three years of more than half a million dollars

"Prepare yourself for jail and the loss of your professional designation. The CRA say you owe them more than $200,000 in taxes. With interest and penalties that will double. How are you going to pay that? You tell me you have no money. You might as well go bankrupt at the same time." This from a lawyer he was paying $350 an hour in advance for advice. On hearing this, Laura began to weep.

"Plead guilty, go bankrupt and be done with it." The lawyer was merciless in driving his point home.

"How can I owe so much money? I lost over a million in businesses that went bankrupt the last two years. That's a write-off I haven't claimed. Our home has been foreclosed and our belongings auctioned off. If I earned that kind of money, how come I couldn't save our home? I have two kids—a one and a three-years-old."

"Alright," sighed the lawyer. "I'll go back to the CRA manager—I worked with him for twenty years before this—and see what they'll settle for." There was not an ounce of sympathy in his voice. All was clinical—a dogged determination to close a losing file for a client who couldn't pay beyond his retainer.

Three weeks later, the lawyer came back. "They'll agree to no taxes, interest or penalties, provided you plead guilty immediately."

"Why would I plead guilty if they say I owe them nothing?" He knew this would be the end of him. He might save $200,000, but his face would be plastered all over the newspapers to frighten other accountants. His professional membership would be expunged. After thirty years in accounting, he would have nothing left—save a wife nearing mental breakdown and two kids, one recently born. He had no choice but to fight.

"I'm not a criminal lawyer, but I can recommend a lawyer who is. She's young and cheap—her rates are far lower than mine."

The word cheap sent alarm bells through him. Cheap was usually synonymous with 'highly inexperienced'. Was she, like his current lawyer, just going to go through the motions? He would end up paying another $50,000 on top of his reassessed tax bill. How was he going to come up with the cash? It was then Laura came to his support. Despite her tears she exclaimed "You're innocent. You have to fight this."

A week later, he was on his way to see Jennifer, his new criminal lawyer.

Calgary was renowned for its downtown streets, chock-a-block full of ultra-modern skyscrapers easily competing with the num- ber New York had. A brand-new law court had been opened recently that rose like a rocket into the sky. Jennifer's address was within two blocks of the Court. He couldn't find it. After asking someone, he was directed to a ramshackle two-storey building about to be demolished and turned into yet another skyscraper. Stairs (not elevators) took him to the second floor. The establishment smelled of dust and more dust. It looked and felt like an attic.

He was ushered into a cubicle-sized room and told to wait.

A five-foot tall, scrawny woman with glasses that magnified her piercing, sky-blue eyes entered. She bore no trace of feminine allure. Her clothes were as non-descript as the comfortable flat shoes she wore. He could discern neither make-up nor clunky jewellery on her to distract attention.

"You're late," were her first words of welcome. There was a grimace to accompany it. "The CRA has sent me five bank- er's boxes of documents and evidence they have against you. Review them all and get back to me. Before I continue with this, I'll need a retainer of $5,000. If this goes to trial, I'll need a further $50,000."

The meeting lasted ten minutes and he had to cart the boxes one-by-one to his car parked five blocks away.

It took him weeks to gather the $5,000 and to screw up his courage and read the files. Opening those boxes was like opening Pandora's Box. He had deliberately kept away from the past, it brought back too many hurtful memories. It also led to despondency and he couldn't afford to become demoralised— his whole family was depending on him.

One morning, as was his custom, he woke up at five and this time, was determined to examine CRA records, while Laura was still asleep.

An hour later, a smile came to his face. A little later, it became a grin and then a guffaw.

The CRA had compiled their version from credit card statements as the banks had closed down his regular accounts because of pressure from his creditors. They had interviewed his clients— old friends who called and told him—and asked for any invoices he had given them. The CRA raided his office and home and took away any records they could find.

Each summer when he was broke, he went to his clients and offered them discounts if they paid their fees in advance. He never took cash. The cheques were deposited into a VISA account. Several months later, when their work had been completed, he issued an invoice stamped as paid.

The CRA took the original deposits then added the subsequent 'Paid' invoices to the total, doubling his income. When CRA raided his home, they went through his garbage bin and extracted a sheet of paper showing sales totalling over $70,000. The CRA added that amount to his income. The sales were clearly marked as belonging to his client, not to him.

Jubilantly, he called his lawyer. "Jennifer, the CRA are wrong. I've caught their errors—and that's only on the income side. I've yet to review their expenses."

There was a roar on the other end. "How dare you call me on my cell phone at eight in the morning. Call me later at my office."

Their second conversation drained him of all his optimism. "OK. Even if you're right, the total income on your credit cards shows over $100,000 a year in income. Your personal tax returns show an annual gross income of $20,000. How do you explain that?"

Correspondence between Jennifer and the CRA stretched to over two years with CRA refusing to budge. They offered the same reprieve. "Admit your guilt and we will reduce your tax reassessment to nil." There was now no alternative but to go to trial.

Little-by-little, he had accumulated enough money to pay Jennifer's monthly bills. It was now crunch time. Where was he going to find $50,000 for the trial? The CRA could be delayed no longer. Jennifer had all but given up on him. Then, a miracle happened. A deal he had been working on for years materialized. His commission came to over $60,000.

Jennifer called him one Friday afternoon. "The trial begins on Monday. We need to meet over the weekend to discuss our strategy. "

"Impossible. I'm in a major Scrabble tournament arranged months ago. I can't get out of it." Silence at the other end of the phone.

"What time does it end?"

"Around 6 p.m."

"Come to my office at seven." She hung up before he could reply.

The Saturday session with her lasted until 11 p.m. She insisted on doing the same on Sunday.

She may have been his defence counsel, but he'd never felt such a wrath of animosity and resentment. How was he supposed to win his tournament with all this distraction? Couldn't they have met earlier in the week? Why leave it to the last minute? She was so much like his mother, whom he'd spent his life sparring with. It was her way or none.

Before starting, Jennifer handed him a two-page letter to read and sign. "You have been advised of the low probability of winning the case and have independently decided to proceed without coercion or misinformation from Jennifer," or words to that effect. It was to protect her from being sued by him in case they lost.

Jennifer began. "The good news is that this is a criminal trial." What good was that? He could go to jail as a result.

"To be found guilty, the CRA has to prove without a doubt that you intentionally lied on your tax returns. If this had been a civil suit, you'd have been found guilty on probability." So much for inspiring confidence in her client.

She went on. "Show up half an hour before the judge arrives at 9 a.m. Do NOT wear your jogging pants, but plain dark dress pants with dark sweater. Don't wear a suit and tie—that's not you. Answer each question truthfully as you are under oath. Answer briefly and to the point. Do not try and justify yourself, unless you're asked. Everything depends on your credibility with the judge. There is no jury. If you prevaricate

99

on each answer, the judge will disbelieve you on everything."

"To save you money, the trial will be cut to three days. To deter the CRA from presenting further potentially damaging testimony, we are negotiating an 'Agreed Statement of Facts'. They have accepted the changes you found. However, we have to admit you showed $20,000 gross income annually, when your deposits show $100,000. They are still disputing your increase in expenses to match your revised income."

A shiver ran through him. "If I admit that, the case is lost, isn't it?"

Her sky-blue eyes pierced through him. "Those are indisputable facts which you, as an accountant haven't disproved." Was there no humanity in her?

His trial began the next day.

The court room had benches like church pews with an aisle down the middle. Jennifer and her client sat to the right. There were no others on their side of the aisle. Laura couldn't bear to come. He had no other support. CRA were represented by their chief prosecutor, a female six-foot-tall with two more female prosecutors to assist her. Behind them, the pews were packed with CRA staff. Among them he recognized the CRA Manager and his assistant. The female CRA investigator, who first found him, was also in attendance. They all had their hair done up and wore their best suits as though attending a wedding. A waft of perfume hung in the air. He wasn't sure whether it was from a male or female.

The Honourable Justice Fairfax arrived an hour late. The defendant was leaning back on his chair with his arms behind his head.

"Sit up straight. Show respect for my court." The judge bellowed at him. The CRA crowd smirked.

Jennifer stood up immediately, presumably to deflect his anger.

"Your Honour, with your permission, can my client sit beside me rather than in his box?"

For a moment, the judge examined him then acquiesced.

The Crown Prosecutor called her first witness: Brenda Smith, the CRA investigator who found him.

"How long were you looking for him?" she rapped.

"More than four years."

"How did you find him?"

"I went to his last known address. His home had been foreclosed. The current owner had some mail for him. One was a newsletter from the Calgary Scrabble Club. It meets every Thursday evening. I went along and found him there."

The judge interjected. "Did you say Scrabble?"

"Yes, your honour."

Taken aback by the judge's question, the prosecutor took a minute to glance at her notes then continued with, "What did you say to him?"

"I couldn't say much. He arrived just as the games were starting. He asked for my business card and promised to call me the next day, which he did."

The prosecutor turned to the judge. "That's all the questions I have your Honour."

It was now Jennifer's turn to cross examine the witness.

"Your honour, I have no questions, but my client has something to say, if it pleases the Court."

The judge peered harshly at the defendant, "What is it now? Stand up."

Hesitantly, he began, "I would like to thank Brenda for her care and concern. Of all the CRA, she was the only one sympathetic to my plight and that of my family. She tried several ways to help us, even suggesting I go bankrupt."

The judge waded in again. "Why didn't you go directly to CRA, agree to the amount you owed and then, if necessary, go bankrupt?"

"Your Honour, I crossed two continents to get to Canada. I didn't come here to claim bankruptcy. I knew that would be the outcome if I approached CRA. I needed time to stabilize my family and then go earn the money to pay my creditors."

"Very well, sit down."

The next witness was the CRA Manager. Dressed to kill, with a golden silk hanky in his pocket, he smiled benignly at the judge.

On a large screen, tax returns for the three years in question were displayed. All showed a taxable income of $6,000 after expenses. the returns were replaced with copies of credit card statements showing annual deposits of over $100,000. Led by the prosecutor, he went through step by step of how CRA had compiled their information and how the defendant subsequently agreed to their revised calculation of his income.

The manager, in a sing-song patronizing manner, fixed all his attention on the judge, emphasizing each telling and damaging aspect of the case. It was obvious he had been a witness many times.

"Get him off the witness stand as fast as you can," he pleaded with his lawyer.

"Do you wish to cross examine the witness?" the judge asked Jennifer.

Her answer was succinct. "No, your Honour."

The Court adjourned for the day. It would be his turn to be questioned tomorrow. Jennifer dragged him through another long and tedious session of prep work.

Finally, arriving home almost at midnight, Laura beseeched him with questions. Thank goodness the kids were asleep. He spent an hour regurgitating the proceedings, trying desperately to be positive for her sake. He went to bed without supper, shattered.

Next day, he was forced to examine each page of each year's tax return.

"Did you knowingly prepare and submit this page to CRA?"

"Yes."

The mantra was repeated over thirty times. "Guilty as sin," he remembered.

There was laughter and guffaw behind the prosecutor. The judge, smiling asked, "Are you all members of CRA?"

The CRA manager returned his smile. "Yes, we are."

Judge Fairfax's face turned to stone. He was livid. "Do you understand a man's future and his family's is at stake? And you're laughing?" The judge beckoned Jennifer to him. His words ricocheted around the courtroom. "Are these people disturbing you? If so, I'll order them to leave."

The judge eyed the CRA manager. "I presided over one of your cases last year. Shaving the next morning, I nearly cut myself. You were on CBC radio criticizing my verdict. You know as well as I do, that if you disagree with my judgement, you need only to appeal, not broadcast your opinions on a breakfast show. If you are dissatisfied with my verdict in this case and I hear you venting the next day on the radio, I will issue a contempt order. Is that clear?"

"Yes, your Honour." The wolf became a lamb. The next day, the manager showed up in dress pants, plain shirt with a leather jacket. No ties, suits or flamboyant dresses could be seen in the CRA camp.

The prosecutor continued. "You are now allocating 60% of your meals on your VISA statements as business expenses. Shouldn't that be 25%?"

"All the meals were for business. The CRA auditor allowed me 60%. I believe his letter is part of the evidence submitted." It was obvious the prosecutor and her staff had ignored that evidence. They were concentrating only on the most blatant and damaging aspects.

"If your expenses were all for business, why did CRA only accept 60%?" The prosecutor tried to draw him out as nefarious.

His frustration boiled over. He rose from his chair. "Have you ever tried dealing with the CRA?" There was a lull as the prosecutor retired to her table and Jennifer took over.

"Did you believe you owed any taxes?" she asked civilly.

"No."

"Why not?"

"In those three years in question, I lost over $1,000,000 from investing in my businesses. We have submitted documents to prove that. I was entitled to write-off three-quarters of that investment against my other income. "

"Why didn't you? "

"Our home was foreclosed on. All our possessions were taken by bank agents and sold at auction, along with all my accounting records. Meanwhile, I had to find shelter and security for my family. We had to live from hand to mouth each day. Yes, I could have gone to the courthouse and searched for the documents to support my claim, but we had no excess cash to do so. Sometimes my wife and I starved in order to feed the children."

Jennifer rattled on. "Are you saying that even if your gross income was $100,000, as an accountant, you believed you had no taxes to pay because of your investment losses you could have claimed? "

"Yes."

Closing arguments were heard and the court adjourned in early afternoon. All expected to be summoned for the verdict within thirty days.

The thirty days rolled into six months and still no verdict.

"We can't go on living our lives in limbo. My wife is beside herself." He pleaded with his lawyer.

There was a pause before Jennifer came back. "There is a way, but it will cost you another $5,000. We can apply for a verdict or, if it's still delayed, ask the Court to throw the case out."

To find the cash to pay Jennifer and then to apply to court, took months. Eventually, a date was set as the judge was still pondering over his verdict.

The day before the hearing, Jennifer called him.

"The CRA have submitted a motion to stay proceedings." She was laughing over the phone.

"What the hell does that mean?" he asked, irritated by her manner.

"The CRA have stated that because the judge took so long and still hasn't reached a decision, the legal action should be stayed. It means that legal action is suspended for a year. In that year, if CRA come across further evidence, they will reinstate their legal action against you. If not, you will be free."

He was perplexed. "Why would the CRA spend hundreds of thousands of dollars and countless man hours pursuing me then drop the case?"

"It may be that CRA believes the judge will acquit you as they didn't prove beyond a doubt that you evaded taxes. If you win they don't want another defendant to use your case in their defence."

A year later, at his acquittal, she vanished from his life as peremptorily as she had entered it.

In Central Park the boys had requisitioned their mum's camera. Imitating the Japanese tourist, they had their mother posing beside Alice, commanding her to raise her fingers, this time in a victory salute. Laughter rang out from all sides.

Within minutes, the weather gods reappeared in their fury. A bitter wind swelled and the sun was swept away behind saturnine, granite-grey clouds. Yet, sunshine suffused his body and soul in gratitude for his deliverance from the storm.

AUTHOR'S NOTE

When The Stars Aligned

It was a David versus Goliath moment.

Nothing could have saved me if one of the following had been missing:

1) The determination of a five-foot tall, 80 pound, female warrior of a lawyer;

2) A judge's sympathy towards me and his animosity towards the CRA manager, the chief, polished witness for the plaintiff;

3) The arrogance of the CRA omitting to do their preparation for the trial, assuming their bullying would win them the case.

Some would call our pyrrhic victory luck, others destiny. I just remember my three guardians angels.

ILLUSTRATOR'S NOTE

I found this story absolutely harrowing from both a personal and business point of view! A real Grimm's fairytale—complete with stormy seas to navigate (personal and legal), heartless wolves (financial) circling for the kill and the desperate hope for justice from on high!

"Finally, they arrived at their destination."

CHAPTER 9
WITH GOD ON OUR SIDE

"IT MUST BE here. It says so in my guidebook."

Laura and the boys stared at him in exasperation. The allure of Manhattan in its Christmas glory had not blunted the edge off the arctic wind blowing in from the Atlantic nor the intermittent snow transmuting itself into rain then, within minutes, returning to its former state.

The four of them had plodded up and down Fifth Avenue between West 54th and 50th Street for an hour.

A vendor sat cross-legged on a thick pad of colourless foam. He and his goods, in this instance postcards of famous sights including St. Patrick's, were laid out on a brightly patterned Persian carpet. His wares rested perilously upon doubled-up wooden cargo pallets to keep them dry from the rivulets of water shooting along the pavement beneath them. Like an Arab nomad sheltering from the blinding desert sun, the vendor held a short pole in one hand supporting a heavy sheet to ward off the rain and snow.

In the week they had been in New York, he was pleasantly surprised by the reaction of vendors across the city. Travelling abroad, vendors were an occupational hazard. Approaching within even yards of one, they would stand up and sing eulogies of their wares, diverting you from your path. In New York, except by the ferry terminal for the Statue of Liberty where they mobbed you to sell ferry passes, tickets and knick-knacks, they left you alone, aloof to the milling crowd, letting the tourists come to them. Which method worked better? For the life of him, he couldn't tell.

"Excuse me. Do you know the way to the cathedral, please?"

"There." The vendor spoke in a rich upper-class Boston accent, pointing to the spot directly in front of him.

"Is that it?" His younger son complained in disgust.

Laura, a stalwart Catholic, loved cathedrals. To humour her, the family had visited and paid respects to a pack of them across the world. Notre Dame could be seen from miles away. The Sagrada Familia rose like the Tower of Babel dwarfing the poor working-class district of Barcelona and attracted ten thousand visitors daily. You couldn't get lost. Simply follow the crowds and stealthily latch onto a group with an English-speaking guide.

Here in New York at six in the evening, on one of its busiest streets, there was no line-up of tourists seeking entrance. And no cathedral.

A small building, wrapped roof-to-floor in scaffolding, stood before them, compressed between gigantic office towers that overwhelmed it. There was no magnificent entryway announcing the whereabouts of a world-famous edifice. From here State funeral services were held and broadcast throughout the world for fallen presidents and leaders, and poet laureates. Yet, here was his family scurrying between jutting poles of scaffolding like drowning water rats.

They entered the dark, dank cavern of worship.

Going inside was much like stepping into the long-abandoned hallway of a castle or stately home in which the windows had been boarded up and the furniture covered over for its own protection. Somewhere he had read St. Patrick's was undertaking a $177 million restoration. The escape from the wet outdoors still left him shivering. The last thing he needed was the cold, comfortless feeling of being enclosed within a crypt. He imagined the smell of dust and decay where there was none. He stared up at the stained glass. The snow-laden grey sky shed no light through the glass to highlight its brilliant colours. What should have been inspirational turned to cold sobriety, leading him to face his own brushes with his now dormant Muslim faith and the great sadness of disappointment they had fostered in him.

He and his Ismaili community came from the once-idyllic harbour town of Dar-es-Salaam—Arabic for Haven of Peace. It nestled on the coast of East Africa gazing out at the endless Indian Ocean. Several generations of his community made up of uneducated shopkeepers and costermongers had, year-by-year, scraped together enough shillings to construct a marble palace as magnificent to them as St. Patrick's was to New Yorkers.

Due to growing intolerance towards East Asians in Tanzania, he was shipped off to England at the age of five to obtain his education. Though not a devout Christian, his foster mother gave him a chain bearing St. Christopher to wear around his neck to protect him on his travels. That first summer back in Africa, the chain was promptly confiscated and replaced by an armband of green cotton thread—the symbol of his community's version of Islam. Each afternoon, he sat in a classroom of five-year-olds—and this when he was twelve—to recite and memorize seven pages of the Koran in Arabic as well as the names of each of the forty-nine past and present imams, the spiritual leaders of his Muslim community. It was his father's everlasting shame and disappointment that each member of his class had led the Jamaat—the congregation—to prayer except his son. It was this force-feeding of religion that first hardened him to his faith.

Despite his abhorrence of those afternoon classes, he welcomed the daily ritual of attending mosque. His father, driving his Vespa, would come pick him up at soccer practice. They would eat a snack of samosas while he guzzled down a bottle of Coca-Cola. Then it would be home to take a shower, put on light grey dress pants and a white short-sleeved shirt. Even in his late teens, he couldn't get away from his father's insistence on combing his short black hair. They walked along the bay and watched the sun go down as they entered their mosque. The glassless windows were opened fully to let in the gentle sea breeze. A girl would mellifluously sing a ginan (hymn). Sitting cross-legged on spotlessly clean rush mats, he found a peace he would spend the rest of his life trying to retrieve.

In the early 1970s, as the internecine tumult spread like wildfire across East Africa, his community fled to England. Their magnificent airy palaces were replaced by ad hoc Friday prayers in derelict warehouses, rented rooms, or church basements where their prayers were drowned out by the Episcopal services from above. Jam-packed among a congregation hurriedly arriving from work, he was overwhelmed by the smell of sweat intermingled with Brut perfume to mask it. The solace of a marble prayer hall and its connection to the Almighty was forever lost.

As his interest and attendance at his mosque waned, he concentrated more and more on studying to become a chartered accountant. On qualifying, the relentless economic crises in England drove him, once again, to seek his fortune elsewhere.

He landed in Calgary as an immigrant for the second time in his life at the age of twenty-four, on a bright, sky-blue, summer-like Tuesday in late April 1980. Unlike many immigrants, he entered as an accepted professional with a job and an apartment waiting for him.

Almost at once, he bumped into fellow accountants, youngsters like him in their early twenties, all Ismaili Muslims also recently emigrated from England, arriving on the skirts of an oil boom in Calgary. He joined them on weekends to play badminton at the Beltline Leisure Centre or watch reruns of black and white movies in the afternoon at the Kensington Plaza.

His friends were never around in the evenings. "We're at prayer. Why don't you join us? After all, you are an Ismaili."

"I haven't been to Jamaat Khana (Ismaili mosque) in years," was his automatic response. It never quite worked to silence them, only make them more determined to persuade him.

One day, weary of their constant banter, he asked them, "What's the most difficult service to perform for our religion?"

They conferred. "The 5 a.m. morning prayer. You live downtown, right? And you have no car? There are volunteers to give you a wakeup call. An Ismaili minibus picks you up and drops you off. There's breakfast afterwards."

"Alright, I'll give it a shot for a month. If it leaves me cold, I'll drop out. And then no more talk from you to persuade me otherwise. Deal?"

They glanced at each other, then nodded their agreement.

On the rare occasions he had attended, especially on Friday nights, Jamaat evening sessions were full of glitz and glamour. For the most part, the congregation was young and smartly attired, the men in suits and ties, the women in formal western dress. He expected his morning Jamaat to be the same. How wrong he was.

Going to mosque in the mornings, he thought he could kill two birds with one stone. He dressed himself in his office suit and asked the driver to drop him at work after prayers. He would have a head start and could finish early to enjoy the summer.

The minibus arrived, packed with what appeared to be unwashed illegal geriatric immigrants. The youngest was the volunteer driver in his early sixties. Men were unshaven. Women wore no makeup. They were garbed in hand-me-downs. He sat gingerly between two of them, ever mindful not to wrinkle his suit tail.

Someone greeted him with "Ya Ali Madat." May the exalted Allah help you. Without a second thought, he replied, "Mowlali Madat." May the exalted Allah help you too. When they continued to converse with him in Kutchi, their native tongue, he couldn't respond. To understand the gist of what was said was doable, but after decades away from the language, he found it impossible to speak it.

Above the body odour rose the tantalizing aroma of dishes his grandmother had cooked for him as a child. Garlic mingled with ginger, cinnamon, and nutmeg—their aroma wafting up from china bowls covered with newspaper—their breakfast he hoped.

As the bus rode off to its next rendezvous, he overheard a smattering of mangled English—"She's a good cooker but she has an inferiority complexion," and "My friends have overtaken my apartment."

Finally, they arrived at their destination.

The prayer hall was pitch black. He could hear the deep arrhythmic sound of snoring. He sat in the dark and waited. Eventually, a voice called the congregation to prayers and the lights came on.

Within a week, because of his English accent, he was honoured with the task to read out past firmans from their spiritual leader, who was based in France and spoke in English to them. Most people from the outside world knew him as the Aga Khan. The firmans themselves were innocuous, urging the congregation to lead a virtuous life and fit into the general society. His father would have nodded with pride. As he read aloud, he pondered over his effect upon his audience. How much of his English was understood by the elderly, Kutchi-speaking members was beyond him.

It was mandatory to start his speech with "Allah huma sale ala Muhammadin wa aale Muhammad." May the praise of Allah be upon Muhammad. He glanced up at his audience. Most had their eyes closed, a number were snoring intermittently. Was anyone listening?

A sudden mischief took hold of him. Instead of saying it once, he continued to repeat the incantation for five minutes, growing ever louder and faster each time, like Ravel's Bolero. Soon, everyone was chanting trance-like, their heads bobbing up and down, bowing to the floor, competing to stay in rhythm, building up to a crescendo. Some faced the door, perhaps, in their fervour, expecting their spiritual leader to appear.

Soon after, he was called before the Mukhi (mosque leader).

Saleem, the Mukhi, was one of his favourites. In his early 30s, he was the youngest mosque leader around. His parents had been given 24 hours to pack and leave East Africa after four generations of being there. The provisions for four members of the family were bundled into one beaten-up suitcase. From that suitcase, a veritable Aladdin's lamp, there emerged one miracle after another. They were flown out of Uganda in the middle of the night and dumped into a transit camp in England. Pierre Trudeau, the prime minister of Canada at that time, was a friend of the Aga Khan. He facilitated the transfer of Saleem, his family and thousands of other desperate and forlorn Ismailis all across Canada. Saleem's family landed in Calgary.

Within a decade, Saleem's stateless, homeless, broken-English speaking family had converted the possessions of that one beaten-up suitcase into the beginnings of an empire which would own auto dealerships, hotels and parking lots, employing hundreds in Calgary.

The Mukhi was chosen from the congregation. He would serve a year then be replaced by another of his flock. He not only had to attend Jamaat Khana seven days a week, he also had to pay for all mosque functions, visit Ismailis in hospital, assist at weddings and funerals and mediate in family disputes. All this on top of his regular secular commitments.

Due to the upcoming Aga Khan's silver jubilee, the Mukhi was asked to stay on a further year to help organize the festivities. There was not one complaint from Saleem. On the contrary, he was genuinely grateful to give back to his community.

The Mukhi reminded him of a Lemur—large endearing eyes, an emasculated body with a face to match.

"Ya Ali Madat," the Mukhi began. "Have you had your breakfast? You are such an excellent reader, what happened to you today?"

Standing in front of the Mukhi, tears welled up. How could he explain he had experienced an epiphany? He had realized what an alien he had become to this mosque and its community. He longed for the peace and tranquility of that marble palace which was forever lost. "I guess I must have fallen into a trance. I haven't been sleeping well."

There was no admonishment. A strange sadness crept into the Mukhi's large, gentle eyes.

He was never again invited to lead or read to the congregation. He survived the month then retired from active service. He had gained no spiritual insight, only the minor satisfaction of silencing his Ismaili friends, who continued to socialize with him bar the cajoling.

St. Patrick's had darkened before his eyes, constricting his thoughts. The boys were peering surreptitiously under dust covers while their mother searched anxiously for an altar to offer her candle and prayers before the cathedral closed. They were alone in this mausoleum to Christianity. How had he gravitated from the marble idyll of his Muslim childhood to this?

After his brief spat with the Jamaat in Calgary, religion never entered his head until he met Laura.

"What are the kids going to be? Catholic or Muslim?" she asked. Coming from a family of seven children, she was determined to have at least two.

His answer shocked him. "Ismaili of course."

She frowned in disbelief, retiring into a shell of silence.

After weeks of her pouting, he came to his senses. He hadn't visited his mosque for years while Laura went to mass once a month and at Easter and Christmas. They lived in the Western world. Roman Catholic schools were academically superior to the state-run schools. Neither he nor Laura had relatives in Calgary. Laura's closest friends were a Filipino family in Calgary. The family was polite, respectful and hardworking— a commendable example to any children Laura and he might have. What would be best for them?

His mother was apoplectic at their decision. The final and, to her, fatal blow fell when he not only sided with Laura but named their boys Alex and Chris, after Alexander the Great and Christopher Columbus. To his mother, it was the greatest betrayal. What was she to tell her fellow congregation?

After this decision, he once again thought everything was settled as far as religion was concerned. But it wasn't.

Alex went on blithely with his life, never taking any interest in Catholicism or any other Word of God.

Chris proved to be a different kettle of fish.

"Pops, my friends are Ismailis. Why haven't you taken me to the mosque? Why haven't you ever told me about your religion?" he asked balefully, as though being kept in the dark about a great family secret.

"Son, we thought it best to focus on one religion so you would have a strong grounding, rather than confuse you with contrasting beliefs."

A few months later, Laura rushed to her husband's side. "Hon,

I was tidying Chris's backpack and found this." She held out a copy of the Koran. "What are we going to do?"

"Nothing. It's wordy and long. He won't get past the first chapter unless you make a fuss and tell him not to read it."

"But he's dating a Muslim," she retorted.

"You married a Muslim and so far, nothing bad's happened to you, has it?" He beamed at her. It didn't help.

He continued. "I'm sure we've instilled enough intelligence and sense into him to make the right decision for himself. Don't panic. Be patient."

Within the sanctity of St. Patrick's, Laura had found a candle to light and an altar to St. Mary to pray for her dead father and younger brother. As she completed her Ave Marias, the boys chorused, "Mum, it's stopped raining. Can we go to the Rockefeller Plaza and skate? It's across the road. We can meet you there."

Observing them with awe, he asked himself how two boys, twenty-one months apart, never babysat, never separated, brought up in the same environment, could be so diametrically opposite in their view of religion, shepherded by two parents—each in their own way—with God on their side.

AUTHOR'S NOTE

How Could You Fault Them?

Having been driven away from the religion of my birth by an overzealous father who, each summer, locked me up with a bunch of students half my age to blindly memorize the Koran, I couldn't believe I was volunteering to attend mosque for a year—at five in the morning.

My cynicism faded at witnessing the sincere caring of the volunteers who called to wake me up, pick me up, feed me and drop me to work.

Not to forget the gentle Mukhi—their leader who instead of berating me for poking fun reading an epistle from the 'pope'—was genuinely concerned I had not eaten my breakfast.

ILLUSTRATOR'S NOTE

Two worlds, two religions, two kids… Learning from your own past and using that experience—along with love and tolerance—to fit the pieces together.

"The miracle arrived as needed."

CHAPTER 10

DEMENTED

FATHER, MOTHER, AND two teenage sons were packed into the grand auditorium of Radio City Music Hall, New York waiting in anticipation for the Christmas Spectacular to begin. Their plush red velvet seats were large and plump with cushioning.

The famous Rockettes—tall lissom girls in skimpy outfits— kick-danced their way, arm-in-arm across the stage. As they completed their routine, each stepped into Santa's sleigh parked to one side. An incredible three-dimensional image saw them driven by Santa and his reindeers across the theatre above the heads of the audience. He jumped up with childish glee to touch the sleigh as it glided overhead.

It was like being in Chox Cinema in its heyday in Africa.

There was no TV in Dar-es-Salaam. Chox was the latest

cinema in an ensemble of a dozen to accommodate a population of 50,000. It was the first modern air-conditioned facility. Chox changed its shows three times a week. His father, head of freight section of East African Airways, made sure the movie reels, flown in from across the world, cleared customs and arrived on time at the cinema week in and week out. For that, Chox awarded him free tickets to all the shows, including a balcony box to avoid the line-ups.

The glitz and glamour oozing out of Radio City was as palpable as that from the stars of the 60s and 70s back home in Africa on grand opening nights. Father and son devoured each star and show as enthusiastically as they did their Canada Dry ginger ale and hot roasted peanuts out of large cones of newspaper. There was Rock Hudson in Ice Station Zebra, Charlton Heston in El Cid, and Peter O'Toole in Lawrence of Arabia.

His Muslim mother divorced his father "an irresponsible bum with no ambition" when her son was five. She was twenty-eight and ostracised by her community for doing so. With neither knowledge of English nor any education, she emigrated to England pulling her only child along with her by his coat sleeve. In England, she migrated from one menial job to another, never giving up on her dream of making millions and being recognized by those in Africa who had shunned her. She realized she couldn't fulfill her goal and take care of her son at the same time, so she found an English family, whom she'd met at work, to foster him.

The family knew nothing of Africa. They could only speak English which, at the age of five, he had never grasped. His knowledge of Swahili, Arabic, Kutchi, Gujarati, Urdu, and Hindi proved totally useless. His mother couldn't afford to pay them. They agreed to look after him for a couple of weeks until his mother found a substitute. The two weeks ballooned into a decade—a miracle which he didn't recognize until he became an adult.

There was no doubt the Asletts loved him. Their stability was practised in strict adherence to a daily schedule. He woke up at the same time each day, ate his meals at the same time, went to school on time and came home for lunch daily. Then, always in bed by 8 p.m. Nothing changed. No change was required.

Then there was Dad.

Though deemed irresponsible, the one promise his father kept was to supply his son with endless free airline tickets to return to Africa each school holiday. For years that ability to return home every three months sustained him through the turmoil of adapting to his new circumstances.

Living with his father for a few months of the year was the exact opposite of his existence in England—no regular sleeping times, eating times or play times—no rules. On weekends, and sometimes even on weekdays, midnight shows ended at two in the morning. Dad had no car, so they walked home across town. If he spotted a car, Dad simply whistled. The car stopped and delivered them home. Dad was popular since infancy. Unlike his son, Dad earned his nickname—Kassare—as a kid playing cricket. It stood for KAssamali SAlehmohamed REmtulla, his full name. Dad was gregarious, fun-loving, generous, and always helpful, whether to release a shipment from customs, purchase an airline ticket under currency restriction or obtain a travel visa.

Dad was also known for his mischief. One summer, his son went looking to purchase a carrom board, a game similar to pool. Trained to economize by his mother, the son walked all over town trying to find the cheapest price. "Dad, can you help me?"

With a twinkle in his eye, his father responded. "Go to Karia-koo—a neighbourhood an hour away—to Dar-es-Salaam Sports House. Ask for Malik, the owner. Tell him I sent you."

In the blistering heat and dust of the afternoon, he trekked all the way to Kariakoo, found the board and Malik and was anticipating a huge discount. "My father's Kassare" he gushed.

"So what?" was the reply. And no discount.

On hearing this account his father burst into laughter. His son retaliated by punching his shoulder. It was okay to join his father in playing tricks on others. Once, they had given Bonamint laxatives, in the form of chewing gum, to his dad's porters at work. They were scooped up and chewed immediately with deep appreciation until the inevitable rush to the toilets and fights over who should go first. It was fun while they practised their black humour on others. It was not at all okay when the son became the butt of his father's prank.

His mothers, both foster and natural, didn't demonstrate their love through hugs and kisses but through discipline to ensure he was safe and prepared for the world. Responsibility was drilled into him. Life was serious business. The hugs came from his father. When there were no cars, his father carried him home on his shoulders. Any residue of laughter and joie de vivre he inherited from his father.

But times were rapidly changing in Africa and not for the better. Once a privileged class in their own right, East Indians were now blamed for a catastrophic downturn in the economy to deflect attention from the disastrous profligacy and socialist policies enacted by the new government—which had fought for independence from British imperialism.

At work, Dad soon found himself the sole East Indian. His friends had all emigrated. At the age of fifty-seven, he discovered that rampant inflation and the bankruptcy of his airline had dwindled his savings to nothing, and his expenses rocketed. Luckily, his son qualified as an accountant and successfully emigrated to Canada. With trepidation, Dad accepted his son's sponsorship to his new country.

But Dad insisted on making his home in Toronto where his friends were, instead of with his son in Calgary, several thousand miles away to the west. Stubbornly, he continued sharing a basement in a dilapidated house, devoting twelve hours a day—including daily travel from one end of the city and back—to manufacturing metal office cabinets in a factory at minimum wage. A decade later his employer went bankrupt and once again, Dad had neither a job or money to eat or pay his rent.

"Dad, come on over. Alex is two and you haven't even seen him. Chris is now nine months old. Laura's already got your bedroom prepared." Finally, Dad succumbed. At the age of sixty-seven, his life was once again in turmoil and flux.

On arriving in Calgary, Dad's first thought was to attend mosque. There, he found more friends from home and sighed with relief. One of them found him a job working the night shift at McDonalds—but it was too hard on him, especially in winter. Another friend encouraged him to switch jobs. This time, the coveted position of a parking lot attendant.

Try as he may, his son couldn't dissuade his father from working. "Dad, why work? At your age, you can go on social assistance. You'll get more than you will working."

His father looked at him askance. "I've worked all my life. Do you expect me to sit in your home watching TV all day? I can work three shifts if I want to, but they're all downtown. Your place is too far away. I can't stand living in the suburbs."

At home, he watched his father slowly disintegrate. Where was his devil-may-care attitude? Glimpses came back when Dad interacted with the boys, as when they watched Minions together. Every Friday, Dad would bring home VHS cassettes from the local video store and introduce Lawrence of Arabia or Thunderball to the boys. It was only then, in those fleeting moments, amid the laughter and excitement of his boys, that he could observe Dad restored to his old self.

Try as he might, Dad couldn't fit into the regime of fixed times and rituals his son had adopted. A month later, he approached his son. "Alnoor lives downtown in a nice apartment and cheap. There's a vacancy. I'm going to join him." And that was that.

On stage at Radio City, tall men dressed as soldiers marched alongside the Rockettes to Tchaikovsky's Nutcracker. The girls wore red and white uniforms, the men immaculate in blue and white. A white castle sparkled in the background. Large snow-flakes fell gently onto the stage. Laura and the boys sat enthralled. Not a word or fidget from them.

Like the soldiers, Dad took particular pride in his appearance. In Africa, his airline uniform never showed a crease or wrinkle. And always, his pilot's cap (though he never was one) sat at a rakish angle atop his head. In Canada, Dad maintained his sartorial elegance wearing blazers, suits, and military ties. His airline cap was replaced by an Irish flat cap. He had the air of having just stepped out of a Fred Astaire movie, always razor-shaved and extravagantly pomaded, not a strand of hair out of place and always bearing the fragrance of Brut aftershave.

Despite working three shifts, Dad never forgot to trudge home to his son once a week laden down with groceries from Safeway and an inordinate supply of English Cadbury's Fruit and Nut and Fry's Turkish Delights for his grandsons. On birthdays, there was always a $50 bill and an ice cream cake from Dairy Queen. They talked for hours about the latest movies he had seen or about his workplace. Dad enjoyed his co-workers and loved chatting with his customers. He was in great form.

December 8th was Dad's eighty-second birthday. It was also his elder grandson's seventeenth. Laura cooked steak—Dad's favourite. He fussed over his birthday cake and insisted on a dozen photos. Dad had mounted old pictures of Alex and framed them with some poetry from Khalil Gibran about children being *"not your own, but arrows shot from your bow."*

Yes, Dad was his usual centre of the party yet... glancing at him surreptitiously, when his mask slipped for a moment, he could trace worry lines and a distracted frown. Next minute almost at the snap of a finger, normal service was restored, and he returned to his original ebullient self. What were his concerns? Since moving out, Dad never shared his thoughts, speaking only of trivialities.

"Dad, you've forgotten to blow out the candles." Dad had been standing up about to blow the two candles in the shape of an 8 and a 2. Suddenly, for no reason, he had withdrawn into himself, lost to his surroundings.

Christmas was coming and the family was looking forward to the Bahamas. "Dad, why don't you come with us?"

"No, son. I have to cover for half a dozen staff. Don't worry, I get double time and lots of tips and presents from my customers. There's also a staff Christmas dinner. Alnoor's on his own too. We'll hit a movie. Stop being a worrywart. Go enjoy yourself. I'll see you when you get back."

Midmorning the next day, he had a call from Laura. "Has Dad called?"

"No. Why?"

"He left his briefcase here. The one that weighs a ton and carries all his rolled coins for work. I've called him several times and left messages on his answering machine. I'm sure he'll be panicking over it. Can you come home at lunchtime and deliver it to him?"

"Sure."

Dad wasn't at home. He tried his workplace. A new person was working at the Eau Claire parking lot. He hadn't heard of Dad. Perhaps he'd been assigned to another lot. He returned to Dad's apartment and persuaded the building manager to take the briefcase for his father. After that, he didn't give Dad much thought. He was too busy clearing his workload before leaving for the Bahamas.

On their return from Nassau, two calls awaited them on their answering machine. None from Dad.

"This is the CIBC bank manager. Could you please call me? It concerns Mr. Kassamali Remtulla."

He called back and caught an embarrassed voice at the other end. "Mr. Remtulla gave you as his next of kin.

"Yes. I'm his son." Concern crept in. What had Dad done now?

"We're not supposed to discuss our client affairs with others, but we're worried about your father. He's such a lovely man." What was going on? Alarm bells began to ring. He hadn't heard from Dad since his birthday. Not even a thank you for his briefcase.

"In the past two weeks, Mr. Remtulla's come in several times to replace his lost debit card. We've reviewed his bank account. He's making at least a dozen transactions a day. Many for only a dollar. Each transaction after the sixth is charged 25 cents. I've waived all past and future bank charges on his account. Is he alright?"

Good question. He thanked the bank manager and returned the second call from Dad's building manager.

"Your Dad was found sleeping in the elevator. He couldn't remember his apartment number."

"But he's been living there for ages."

"Yes, I know, but still. We're scared he's going to be robbed. He always carries wads of money around with him. He's going to be beaten up or worse. He's such a lovely man." If he heard Dad being described as "a lovely man" again, he'd scream. The caretaker was from Chile. He could sense the man's unsaid condemnation as if to say, "back home, we'd never treat our fathers that way."

"I've tried to cover up for him, but the tenants have complained. He has until the end of the month to leave. I'm sorry, I can't do any more." His gruff Spanish accent melted in sympathy.

What could he do?

"We have to go find him," Laura said.

They convinced the building manager to let them into Dad's apartment.

Dad got himself a two-bedroom. He had never allowed them in before, giving vague excuses to put them off. The whole of apartment, bedrooms, the dining room, and sitting room were crowded with boxes. There was no room to sleep except for one half of a couch, on which rested two wafer-thin pillows and several blankets laid on top of each other. The thermostat wasn't working. The gauge remained on max, forcing them to discard their coats and sweaters while they fiddled around trying to reduce the heat. A centimetre of dust lay across every surface. The place smelled of rotting food and Vick's menthol rub.

The boxes he examined were chock-a-block full of old 649 lottery tickets stretching back for years. While living in Toronto, his friends persuaded him to enter their lottery pool. They won... a minor prize. Dad's share was $30,000. To him, it was a fortune. Since then, Dad's life mission was to win a major prize. He must have repaid his winnings in full, with interest. Part of his strategy was to use numbers he gleaned from his meanderings. The car registration numbers from his parking lot, serial numbers from grocery receipts were all indexed and filed in date order in one box after the other, with lottery application sheets stapled to them.

In one corner of the dining room lay a pile of unopened mail: a demand from his landlord—he was two months in arrears, a letter of termination from his employer (just before his birthday) phone and cable bills all overdue.

"Why didn't we spot this?" he asked Laura.

"Because you were too busy or too annoyed to ask him or take the time to step back and figure things out." Laura was Dad's staunchest ally. He had quickly accepted her as his daughter, while others asked, "Why marry a Filipina nanny? Couldn't you find a nice Muslim?" They never took into account that Laura graduated with two degrees and was working for a major bank before retiring to look after their boys full time.

Finally, they heard a key turn in the lock. Dad entered. He looked like a hunted animal. His eyes widened like a deer caught in a headlight. "What are you doing here?"

He was unshaven, no tie, shirt collar open, buttons missing. He appeared to have slept in his clothes. His suit was wrinkled and creased.

They were as startled as he was. Who was this man?

Husband and wife spoke together. Dad couldn't hear them. Since his school days, when teachers slapped him about the ears, he was nearly deaf. Powerful hearing aids had saved him. Now they had disappeared. He stared at his father then at his wife, wondering what to do.

Laura came to the rescue. She found a pen and, on the back of an envelope wrote We're taking you home with us.

Dad was petrified. He began to tremble. "I don't want to go. This is my home."

She wrote again. Only for tonight to babysit the boys. Dad acquiesced.

Next morning, he was on the phone to Calgary Social Services to make an urgent appointment.

By the afternoon, Dad and he were seated before a prim, spectacled female in her late thirties.

She asked Dad his name and date of birth. Dad looked beseechingly at his son. He took both hands and pointed them at his ears then rotated his wrists indicating he could neither hear nor understand her.

Dad was given a written eight-question test. He threw it away, withdrawing into a corner repeating, "I don't know. I don't know. I want to go home."

The assessor asked, "Do you have guardianship or power of

attorney over your father?"

"No."

"We can do nothing without a doctor's letter attesting to his physical and mental capacity. We can't test him as he's deaf. How long has he been like this?"

"Don't know. We were away for Christmas in the Bahamas."

She gave him a sardonic look. "There's a three-year waiting list for accommodation at a seniors' lodge. Even longer for a locked facility for dementia."

"We can't wait that long. He's been given an eviction notice. He has three weeks to move out. He can't stay with us. "

A few hours ago, he had slipped out to meet a client, leaving Dad snoozing in the sitting room while Laura cooked in the kitchen. Within minutes of his leaving, Dad woke up, opened the door and wandered out into the street. It took Laura an hour to find him.

Because of his deafness, Dad had an astonishingly loud voice. "I want to go home. Take me home," he repeated.

"Get a letter from your father's doctor recommending a mental assessment. Have your father sign making you his legal guardian and giving you his power of attorney. You are his only child?" As she asked, he glanced at his Dad regretting, for once, that he had no siblings to turn to.

Dr. Mitha had treated them for years. He had also come from Dar-es-Salaam and had known his father since then. The doctor completed his recommendation within the hour.

Ali, his lawyer, had been a close family friend for decades. He came to their home and spoke to his father. Dad didn't recognize him. When would he stop recognizing them? With infinite patience, in brief moments of lucidity, Ali managed to have Dad sign the necessary documents. With a stroke of a pen, Dad handed total control of his life and being, irredeemably, to his son. Gone was the freedom he had clung to all his life.

Dad had no will. He possessed no assets of monetary worth.

Within a week, he guided his father through a battery of tests, got his teeth fixed, hearing aids ordered and made sure he had the medicine to retard his dementia.

Coming home one evening after a day of errands with his father, he gave Laura a progress report. "They've placed Dad on an emergency waitlist. There's nothing more we can do, save pray they find him a place to stay. It'll be a miracle if they do. We still need to clear out his apartment. I don't want to do so until he's moved out. It'll break his heart."

Dad had been staying with them for almost a week. He hardly spoke of his apartment. He was in constant melancholia. He sat in front of their bay window staring out at the snow-covered garden (even though it was March). Suddenly, for no reason, he would burst into tears. The only time he smiled or became animated was around his grandsons. As soon as he saw them on their return from school, he would shout "Boys. Boys." He couldn't remember their names, but he still remembered Laura's name and his own son's.

The miracle arrived as needed.

Social Services called. "We have a vacancy at Cedars. Please call them. You have twenty-four hours to inspect the home and approve."

They left Dad with a neighbour and dashed off to Cedars.

It was a sprawling low-lying bungalow affair just off the main road, barely fifteen minutes away. It was old and shabby. The staff were from every third world nation except their supervisor—an Irishwoman close to retirement herself. She didn't smile, giving the impression they were eating into her precious time.

What could they do?

At ten the next morning, they brought Dad along together with a stash of clothes, suits, and blazers on hangers.

"He won't need those suits. Nor underwear. He'll have diapers. If you can, buy some jogging pants and non-slip runners. Make sure they have Velcro tabs, not laces. No jewellery or other valuables. We'll need a list of his medication and schedule of taking them."

When they left him, it was like leaving their kid at preschool on his first day. There were tears and assurances that they would be back.

"Dad, you're only here for a few days for a check-up. We'll be back tomorrow."

For the first few weeks, each day when they visited, his clothes were piled high on his bed. Coats and jackets on hangers crowned the mound of raiments. On waking up, the first thing Dad did was ready himself for leaving.

"Boys? Boys?" Dad shouted as soon as he saw them. His hearing aids still hadn't come. Consequently, his voice boomed a hundred decibels over everyone else's. They felt sorry for dad's roommate, a gentle soul who always smiled but never said a word.

Summer turned to autumn then to winter.

Back at Radio City, he heard the sound of clapping. The kids had seen Minions on stage. The little yellow creatures, spouting gibberish had been the joy of Dad and the boys who watched the movie together over and over again. During Dad's stay at Cedars, the boys had spotted a large poster full of bright yellow Minions against a sky-blue background and fetched it for their grandfather, taping the poster to the wall so he could see it every day.

Their daily visits to Dad turned into rituals as they stopped at the canteen to buy Coca Cola and a Kit Kat—his favourites.

Sister O'Reilly, in charge of the ward, made sure each resident was given enough attention by the staff. She still found the time to chat with Dad's visitors and give them an update.

One afternoon as the wind chill of -40C ushered him into the ward, he heard Sister O'Reilly's voice. The cold wind had frozen his breath onto his spectacles, temporarily blinding him.

"You said you wanted Kassare on your dad's door? He's complaining. He wants us to change it to Remy.

"That's what they called him at the parking lot."

A day later, she came to them again. "Your dad keeps raiding the freezer for ice cream."

It was Laura's turn to smile. "Like father, like son." She poked his stomach.

Weeks later, Nurse O'Reilly rushed to their side, her face struggling between laughter and a frown. "Remy tried to escape. He waited at the door and followed a couple out."

He recoiled. "How did they find him?"

"He asked the receptionist to order him a cab."

Dad's first anniversary at Cedars came and went. By now, he

considered himself King of the Walk. He had made so many friends and was back to his old gregarious self. It helped that, little-by-little, his medication had been modified for the better. Once again, he hid his hearing aids. But eerily, he seemed to understand what was being said to him. Was he lip-reading? Son took father roaming in a wheelchair up and down the hallways. Every now and then, Dad hailed someone or other by name. Whether it was their real name or not, his son never found out, too embarrassed to ask.

On another day, an orderly came up to them, perplexed. "Remy asks for paper and pencil. Then he looks out at the parking lot, taking down the auto licence plates."

Smiling, he answered, "At the end of each shift at his parking lot, Remy always prepared a list of car plates that were still parked and handed them over to the next shift worker."

One Sunday morning, a month after his father's anniversary, he went on his own to visit Dad. He was sleeping, emitting a soft snore. For once, Dad was at peace. It was such a relief not to see his clothes piled up on his bed ready for him to leave. That he had created the same environment around him of people he could connect to who liked him too. And that he was suffering no pain.

It was time to leave. He left the usual snacks beside Dad's bed and told the nurse he would return later.

"Could you buy him another pair of sweatpants?" she asked.

"Sure. I'll bring them this evening."

He took Laura to church, then to Dim Sum at the Regency Palace in Chinatown. From there, they headed out to Chinook Shopping Mall and Hudson's Bay to buy Dad's pants.

His phone rang.

Later, he couldn't remember the words he'd heard, save a gentle, sympathetic voice telling him, "Your Dad died in his sleep."

An ocean of memories drowned him—Dad on that blessed Vespa picking him up from soccer practice in Africa, evenings spent buying luscious fruit and snacks outside their mosque in Dar-es-Salaam. Dad's overwhelming zest and joy of living, turning the most very mundane of tasks or meetings into something so special.

He compared his own disciplined methods in bringing up his children to those of his freewheeling father. He wondered how much joy he had instilled in his boys—sadly, a pittance of what his Dad had bestowed on him in those precious months each year in Africa.

In the middle of the store, Laura wept inconsolably. No tears came to him.

Wild, dissonant clapping yanked him back to Radio City. He was the only one sitting. Laura and the boys were cheering for an encore. He still hesitated to stand up. Tears that once would not flow, cascaded down his cheeks. Dad would have loved the show.

AUTHOR'S NOTE

A "Real Angle"

While in Africa, my Fui, the sister to my father, fed all the stray, undernourished cats in her neighbourhood. She arrived in Toronto, then was stranded at home with no understanding of English while her children left for work—so she created a job of her own.

Writing in Gujarati, she prepared a list of elders isolated at home. She never failed to call them each day and cheer them up with her infectious joy for living. Like my Dad, she too had the most beautiful wide-mouthed smile, her large teeth glittering white.

On her death, my father, with his usual penchant for typos, praised her as a "real angle".

My father too was a "real angle". It wasn't writing about him that brought tears to my eyes, but the way Lorie, my illustrator, brought him to life—the dazzling smile, his "air pilot" outfit, riding his Vespa nonchalantly into the sunset

I didn't realise how much I missed him until then. Nor how much I missed my Fui.

Thank you, Lorie.

ILLUSTRATOR'S NOTE

I read a quote once that said "...the landscape of our childhood becomes the landscape of our dreams."

Good or bad—our memories of the places and people we knew as children, often loom 'larger-than-life'.

"In our culture, a son always pays for his mother…"

CHAPTER 11

BLIND

MANHATTAN, OR IN the language of the Lenni Lanape, "Mana-hata" meant "island of many hills". Today, the many hills had sprouted into innumerable skyscrapers disappearing into the clouds—the modern-day version of urban hills. If only the weather had been more forgiving, he might have learned to love this city. Looking back, he could easily have said the same about life and what it had bestowed upon him.

Despite the snowy fogbound windblown December weather, for a few hours he was free again—perhaps for the last time in the city, prior to returning home with his family. While they slept that morning in their hotel room he visited his favoured haunts—collecting French pastries from Petrossian for his wife and sons and then perhaps a farewell visit to Argosy, the antiquarian bookstore. He might discover more of those out of print books he had read as a child, whiling away summers in East Africa.

Within the ultra-modern walls of the skyscrapers looming down at him, there was a touch of Grand Bazaar or some major crossroad of the Silk Road. Treasures from every corner of the world and from each era of history could be found, imbuing their sterile cells with the magic of civilization. All you had to do was look.

His mother would have commended the choice of New York as a destination, be it for its men and women so fashionably dressed, or the glamour of Bergdorf Goodman. In England, Harrods was her Mecca. She could afford nothing but a salt-shaker on sale from its basement, but she would travel the thirty miles by train from Maidenhead each sales season to secure the free half-a-dozen Lincoln-green plastic bags that she demanded with her purchase, with the imprimatur of Her Majesty the Queen emblazoned in gold lettering along with the royal coat of arms. She wore these proudly on her arm, instead of the haute couture she could ill afford. One day, when she became rich and famous, she would charge into the store to acquire the most expensive mink and perfume.

What made someone with no education, speaking rudimentary English (she had emigrated from Africa penniless several years prior), working a string of menial jobs to survive, divorced with a child of five dragging her down, have the audacity to believe that one day she'd be "somebody"?

Mum's father had been a professional card sharp operating in the dingy back streets of Dar-es-Salaam, on the seashore of East Africa. One night, he made a killing. Coming home later, he himself was killed and robbed leaving his wife to bring up six children, none older than twelve.

As a child, he'd heard stories of his nanima (grandmother) throwing kilogram metal weights at her children to keep them in order. Her absolute discipline and purpose produced kids who, each in their own way, became financial successes but seemed to carry the world on their shoulders with all the seriousness of Puritans. Bit-by-bit, through a sharp tongue and continuous carping, they deserted her one by one, leaving her bedridden within the confines of a large ground floor apartment to be cared for by a troop of African servants.

On returning home to Africa each summer, he made a point of visiting his nanima daily. She rewarded him with an outpouring of love she never showed her own children. Nanima regaled him with stories of her past whilst ordering her servant to bring forth a Primus stove so she could lean over and cook her grandchild his favourite dishes.

To escape the hell of her family, at the age of twenty, his mother married a young charmer of her own age who worked for East African Airways. It was physical love at first sight between two volcanic personalities. He was born a year into their marriage. Four years later, she divorced "the bum with no ambition who always wanted a good time and spent all his money" and escaped to England, yanking her son along with her. She was twenty-six years old.

The streets of Manhattan always surprised him. Walking along Madison Avenue, past Minamoto Kitchoan, a Japanese confectionery shop, he ventured onto a side street. A Persian rug emporium caught his attention. Several years ago, in London, while his family slept, he came across a mews off Brompton Road. The mews, once an alleyway housing stables, had been converted into artisan workshops. One of them displayed a silk rug of intricate royal blue patterns, interwoven with gold thread. It was a small rug, perhaps three by six foot. He entered and asked for the price–nine thousand pounds (twelve thousand dollars). No, thank you. And now, here it was again in New York. Dare he ask the price? He quickly walked on to avoid the temptation.

In England, Mum couldn't look after him. An English family she met at work agreed to take care of him while she worked and schemed to make her millions. Once a week for an hour she visited him, berating him for not doing his homework (his working-class family banned the practice—too much learning was never good for you) and exhorting him, at the age of five, to conquer the world.

At fourteen, she pried him from them. "I don't want you to turn Christian. You're an Ismaili." Once she made up her mind, she could not be turned. She removed him instantly with the aid of the police, divorcing him yet again from a loving and secure environment.

Mum had now progressed from being a cleaner to a position as a full-time bookkeeper during the day and a hotel auditor by night. She left him notes on the fridge and wads of money to go wherever he pleased, to eat and watch shows in London without her. Sunday afternoons were the only times they met in person.

Despite Mum's frugality, her mania for saving, and "spending wisely", she never stinted on him. When his father sent him a TWA ticket to fly around the world for two months but no money to pay for his expenses, Mum stepped into the breach. In his final year, Burnham Grammar School offered a Mediterranean cruise on SS Nevasa visiting historical sites. The trip cost sixty pounds. Mum never hesitated nor complained.

By the time he completed high school, she had saved enough to buy a flat. A year later, she sold it making more in profit than from all her jobs in a year.

Meanwhile, he became the incorrigible failure of her life—"just like your Dad". He was supposed to graduate from Oxford or Cambridge yet failed his high school exams. She forced him to learn to drive. It took 364 lessons for him to pass. He was interested in one thing—she in another. But it was always her way and no other.

Looking back, her powerful personality and propensity to dominate left two options to their relationship. He could capitulate and bow to her every wish and whim, or fight tooth and nail against all she laid down.

He refused to retake his school exams. A family friend got him into articling with a firm of Chartered Accountants. She breathed a sigh of relief. Finally, he was off her hands.

Suffering five years to qualify, he promptly emigrated to Calgary leaving his mother to her real estate empire in England. Ten years passed, with barely any communication between them.

It was 1990 and the Queen was coming on a Royal Visit to Canada. By then, the upheaval in Africa had spewed out his family of aunts and uncles all across Canada, except Calgary— the very reason for his choice of destination.

His maternal relatives bombarded him with letters. His uncle in Toronto called him. He was Mum's favourite. "Your mum wants to visit Canada and follow the Queen's itinerary. It's about time you invited her over, after all she's done for you." His uncle loved to chew Paan—a mixture of herbs, spices and shaved betel nuts wrapped in a leaf the shape of a mini samosa. On the phone, he still seemed to be chewing and occasionally spitting out the remains then returning to chewing again. Unfortunately, if you partook in this exercise regularly, your teeth turned bright red from the ingredients. As his uncle spoke, he could picture red spittle dribbling out of the corner of his mouth.

"Why can't she see the Queen in England?" he countered. "After all, they're practically neighbours at Windsor Castle. Has she made an offer on it yet? Think of the money she'll save staying at home and watching the tour on telly."

The Buddha of Suburbia was not amused. "It's about time you grew up and supported her in her old age."

"But she's worth ten times what I am," he retorted in exasperation.

There was more hawking on the other end of the phone. He could picture his uncle spitting out the rest of his paan before delivering his lecture to his wayward nephew. "In our culture, a son always pays for his mother. You're not only the elder son, you're her only child." The unspoken words "shame on you" hung in the air.

He relented. It was the worst mistake in his life.

A few weeks later, he called his uncle back. "Okay. I've organized a travel programme for Mum across Canada. I can pay for the airfare and her pocket money, but she'll have to stay with each of you. I don't have a car, not even a bed. I live in a bachelor suite downtown. The Queen's visit ends here, so Mum can stay with me for a few days on her way back to England. Perhaps she can hitch a ride back with Her Majesty."

In England, Mum lived in a posh suburb, in a maisonette filled with sumptuous furniture and antiques she had collected over the years. Mum owned a Toyota and drove to London frequently to shop and attend her mosque in Kensington. His apartment was the size of a motel room, furnished only with an Ikea folding table, one rickety office chair, a sleeping bag for himself with a boom box to play his cassettes of classical music. There was no TV. He borrowed a mattress for his mum from his close friend Eddie, a wealthy, semi-retired, sixty-year-old. Mum would have to use public transport and learn to walk again. Now in her early 60s, he hoped she could withstand the stress of living his lifestyle. He prayed the week would soon be over.

Dutifully, he planned the week out, scheduling Eddie to whisk them off to Banff, their local mountain resort, or stocking up his fridge with foodstuffs and snacks he thought his mother would enjoy. The moment she stepped off the plane from Vancouver, she tore the whole plan to shreds.

"I want an ice cream," she demanded, even before Eddie and he had retrieved her luggage. They took her to Confetti, his favourite ice cream parlour in the Greenview Industrial Park.

She crinkled her nose at the area.

"Mum, they have fifty varieties of ice cream. Try the guava." She chose vanilla.

She had no time for Banff, wanting to inspect show homes and houses for sale instead. "Look at the price of property here. It's so cheap compared to Maidenhead. This place is booming. I could make a fortune here. Why are you renting? You're such a waster, just like your Dad."

Mum gorged herself on steak and salmon. "The food is so cheap. At home it costs triple. And the quality!" she waxed lyrical.

He had avoided his mosque for years. She demanded a visit to each of the three mosques in Calgary, attending every evening along with her son. She was on the lookout for long lost cousins from out of Africa she'd last seen in 1959.

For some reason, she never complained about her floor mattress or the lack of a TV to watch her news programmes. Nor that she had to sleep inches away from her son. He barely got two hours sleep each night as she returned to her old habit of preaching to him about conquering the world.

Now he was worried whether he could withstand the stress of living Mum's lifestyle. His heart began to miss a beat.

The Queen arrived in a swirl. The only public gathering was at the Olympic Plaza in front of Calgary Town Hall at 11 a.m. Mum took the C-train to see her. He had a job to go to.

Her Majesty came and went. But not his Mum. Her week soon to end, she extended her stay a further month.

It was more of the same. Someone at the mosque told her to shop at Value Village, way up in the Northeast. Her friend had discovered a pair of second-hand vintage Levi jeans for ten dollars, reselling them for $200 to a Japanese collector.

Her birthday came. He had a special Filipino cake baked for her—a purple yam cake, layered in strands of coconut dyed in green. She thought he was trying to poison her and refused to eat a bite.

"Where's my Black Forest Cake?" she boomed.

Finally, she left, but the damage wasn't over.

A week later, he received another call from the Buddha in Toronto. "Your Mum wants to emigrate to Calgary. You need to help her."

"What's she going to do here in the middle of winter stuck in a one-bedroom apartment without a car? It's madness. Why can't she go to her siblings in Vancouver? Anyway, she's happily settled in England."

Once again, he heard the tone of an adult chastising a child. "She wants to be with you. She sacrificed so much for you. She wants to spend what's left of her years with you."

He had flown eight thousand miles to get away from her, now she was coming back into his life like a homing pigeon to plague him once again. She had relatives all over Canada, yet she chose Calgary—the one city where she knew no one, save for him. What was he going to do? Pray he could convince her to emigrate to Vancouver.

Mum was adamant that Calgary would be her home.

It took three years to sponsor her. Typical of her, she chose April 30th to arrive, the busiest day in the year for accountants, being the deadline to file personal tax returns. Did she do this on purpose? Or was this part of the twisted Karma they shared? He couldn't tell. He got her a one-bedroom apartment in his building and introduced her to his friends—Ismaili Muslims and Jews alike. Eventually, he introduced her to his Filipina girlfriend Laura.

He took Mum to the Golden Inn Chinese restaurant by their apartment. Mum ordered pan-fried Dover sole—her favourite— as they waited for Laura to arrive from work.

On seeing her, Mum flared up. "Why can't you marry a decent Ismaili girl? Why a Filipina nanny? Gormless as usual. I bet she's using you to pave her way into Canada. Anyway, I can't see why she'd want you—no house, no car, no furniture. What do you do with your money? Throw it away like your father?"

"Laura works at CIBC, one of the largest banks in Canada. She has two university degrees and got her Canadian citizenship on her own before we met."

"It won't last," was Mum's final comment.

He could feel all her jealousy and possessiveness pour out of her. Vindictive to the nth degree, he knew Mum would direct her wrath at Laura, who would take it all in without a murmur.

In the oppressive heat of the restaurant cocooned in its intrinsic smells of ginger, fried fish and smoke, there was the ever-present clatter of plates being served or taken away. In his attempt to defend Laura, both their voices rose. Other patrons cast sidelong glances at them. Laura sat ramrod straight and wordless. Tears rolled down her cheeks. Bennie, the waiter he'd known for years, came up to them and hesitantly asked if everything was all right.

A year later, when he married Laura, Mum refused to attend. Laura and he moved into a two-bedroom condo, still in downtown, but far enough away from Mum. A few months later, Laura became pregnant. In her last trimester, they bought a brand-new Toyota. Laura and their new baby would need transport, especially in December, their son's due date.

He drove the car to Mum to show her. "We finally have a car. A blue Corolla, your favourite colour. Didn't you always drive one in England?"

She stared at him frigidly for a moment then walked back into her lobby without a word.

From then on, she would call him daily for a ride. "Can you take me to the mosque? I had to give my car up to come here."

"Mum, I've a doctor's appointment for Laura and baby Alex. You live in a building full of Ismailis. There's a mosque bus that comes to the door to take them and bring them back. All you have to do is be in your lobby on time."

"I wish I'd stayed in England. The only time I ask for help and you refuse."

"Alright, I'll be there."

Twenty minutes later, after abandoning his family to go to her, Mum called back. "It's fine. I got a ride. "

He wanted to scream. She did this to him all the time until one day, he had an idea.

The next time Mum asked, he arrived promptly without demur. "What do you think of our new nameplate?" He had spent $173 to purchase the personal licence plate "Kassare"— his father's beloved nickname.

Mum shot off like a rocket. Her rage resembled that of the Red Queen in Alice in Wonderland—"Off with his head" would have been her preferred order of business.

"Is this some kind of a joke?" she demanded. "After all your father did to us? Did you ever think I would sit in a car with his name on it?"

A huge smile emerged across his face.

Two years later their second son, Christopher, was born. They built a home on Signal Hill—an up-and-coming suburb—on half an acre of land with a panoramic view of the city. He brought Mum to see it, but before she reached the front door she exclaimed "Don't like it."

Driving her back, he asked, "Mum, what's there not to like? It's five thousand square feet, brand new and built to our specifications. You always complained I had no car nor owned a home.

Well, here it is. And it's spectacular. Aren't you happy for us?"

She grimaced.

As the years passed, Mum showed no interest in his kids except to put them down. They were scrawny. Why on earth did he call them Alex and Chris? He was an Ismaili.

Eddie called him one day. "I don't want anything to do with your mum again." It was a shock. Eddie would do anything for anyone.

"I was coming back from Bowness and saw your mum waiting for a bus, so offered her a ride. Instead of going home, she made me visit people all over town. She's buying and selling second-hand furniture from home. She didn't even thank me but asked me to pick her up again tomorrow."

He visited Mum soon after. A couple of students came looking to buy a small Ikea coffee table she was selling for $60. She showed them an old Ikea magazine with its price at $80. "Look," she declared. "It's like brand new. No marks. And you're saving yourselves $20."

Feeling sorry for the kids, he butted in, "Why are you showing them last year's magazine?" He picked up the latest magazine tucked in under a sofa pillow." This year the table's on a special price of $40."

She stared daggers at him.

The students looked at each other. "Thanks. We'll think about it."

On their leave, he got a mouthful of invective of how he was ruining her business when she needed every cent to survive. If he couldn't be useful, he should go back to his wife and leave his mother alone.

Verbal abuse from Mum towards his family escalated. She knew exactly what to say to reduce Laura to tears. Insult upon insult— she couldn't dress properly, couldn't be trusted, her cooking was the pits—she couldn't cook Indian food or even a decent steak.

If only Laura would retaliate. But she didn't. After ten years of marriage, she still couldn't find her voice. It was time for him to make a choice. His family or his mum.

Snow and biting wind started up again as he turned left off Madison Avenue towards Central Park and proceeded past The Plaza Hotel towards his family staying at the Marriot Essex House, a few blocks down. A small storefront, barely ten feet wide, caught his eye. Through a window beside the entrance he spotted a work of art.

Two summers ago, he was wandering around Place des Vosges in Paris, an ancient square where Victor Hugo wrote Les Misérables. The grand houses had been turned into outdoor bistros and art studios. One of them espoused a modern artist. He had created a diorama, a three-dimensional vista of Paris using cardboard shapes cut out to represent Paris icons such as the Eiffel Tower. The cardboard pieces were intricately paint- ed then laminated. They were placed together, some behind the other in an upward sweep culminating in the Basilica of Sacré Coeur in the background. In this Manhattan gallery, the same artist had created a three-dimensional panorama of New York City including its famous yellow cabs in the foreground. The abundance and breadth of goods and art displayed in New York astonished him. There was nothing he could not find from any corner of the world.

The belligerent weather induced him to enter the mini gallery, ostensibly to ask the price of the artwork. It was $3,600 USD.

For a moment he hesitated, debating its purchase. Then, sadly, departed into the unforgiving cold.

Ten years passed with not a word communicated between his mother and him. Through the grapevine, he heard Mum had bought a car and a condo and was back dabbling in real estate. A mosque leader called. "Your Mum has glaucoma. She's almost blind. She refused to see a doctor, leaving it too late to cure. She wants you."

His first instinct was to refuse. "Can I call you back? I'd like to think it over."

There was no way he wanted to see her again, falling into the same old rut of reopening wounds that still festered. Yet Chris had been nagging him every time his grandmother's name came up.

"You never let me see her."

Chris so dearly wanted to get acquainted with his past. The only relative they had in Calgary was his grandmother. He was too young when they severed their relationship with her to understand why. Chris would forever blame him if she died and they never met. Perhaps it was time. She might treat Chris as lovingly as Nanima had treated him all those years ago.

"Alright, YOU go and see her. Your mum will drop you. Call her when you're done."

"It won't be for a while. I've taken the whole day off to be with her. I hope she has some old family photos to show me."

First, she didn't want to see him, she wanted to see his father. Each time Chris took a day off to be with her, she changed her mind. She wasn't feeling well. Could they make it another day? And on it went. Chris never gave up on her, showing a patience his father never had. A week of negotiations took place before his mother finally capitulated.

The day arrived.

Laura dropped Chris off and returned home, not expecting to hear from him again until suppertime.

Piecing the story together from his wife and son, Chris called within the hour. "Mum, can you fetch me?"

As soon as Chris got in the car, she asked, "What happened?"

"I don't ever want to see her again. She wouldn't buzz me in. Instead, she climbed down three flights of stairs to open the door for me. They don't have an elevator in her building. Grandma is completely blind. She clutched the stairs as she brought me up, counting each step aloud to herself. She knew exactly where she was. She didn't want any help from me."

Laura asked, "Did she tell you about Daddy and his past or show any pictures of him as a boy? Did she ask what you and Alex were up to?"

"No. She said it was a waste of time talking about the past. Instead, she gave me a batch of Safeway grocery receipts to read out to her. Someone had gone shopping for her. She wanted to make sure they hadn't cheated on her. Then she told me off because I read too slow."

As he heard the story, he couldn't stop thinking of Joe, his ex-boss in Calgary. Joe had also been domineering and controlling. On being told he was going to lose his sight, Joe committed suicide. Look at how Mum fought her infirmity. What made her fight on, battling like a tiger to the end?

There was no further communication until the call from the lawyer several months later.

"I'm sorry to inform you your mother died yesterday. Her funeral's on Friday."

"I won't be attending."

So much anger engulfed him. So much antagonism. He remembered being extricated from his African community, then again from his English family. He remembered her mad quest for glory and recognition at whatever cost. She had presented him with a metaphoric handbook of how NOT to bring up a family. Even now, his first memory of his parents was his Mum, five-feet-tall, throwing a pot of rice at his father.

For decades, he had veered away from any thought of marriage, afraid of what it would bring... And then Laura stepped into his life and over their two decades together, they had rewritten the rules.

The lawyer interrupted his thoughts. "She left you three million dollars."

"Whaat!" Anger seized him again. For years, Mum had sent intermediaries asking him for financial support. All her investments had soured. She needed $1,200 per month from him to survive. He could not refuse. He remembered all those years of his own family's hardships. Of losing their home and business, of the desperation and determination to see their children through private school and then on to university, the continuous struggle to support Mum—like a perpetually throbbing and growing abscess. WHY? If she had all those assets, mostly in cash according to her lawyer, why did she put him and his family into such financial jeopardy to support her?

The lawyer answered, "In her last years, she spent little on herself, hoarding it all for you. To establish a retirement fund in case anything went wrong in your life."

The snow subsided as he entered Essex House. Suddenly, he stopped, hesitated for a moment, then about turned, to make his way back to the little art gallery beside The Plaza Hotel. As he did so, he heard his mother's voice howling in the wind, "A frivolous waste of money."

AUTHOR'S NOTE

My Mum will be ninety next Wednesday, August 10, 2022.

Because of her dementia and blindness, she is in a large private room in a brand-new Ismaili facility. She is surrounded by people of her own faith and language.

Despite the 120 or so active volunteers, I have hired two Ismaili women in their early 60s to tend to her seven days a week. To feed her, pray with her and keep her company.

Recently, I bought her a large fan, just in time for the heat wave we are experiencing in Calgary.

Her birthday is arranged: a cake, delicious Gulab Jamun, her regular calls to her sister Saker in Montreal and her favourite younger brother Fateh in Toronto, if she is able.

That fiery dragon now weighs 72 lbs, sleeps for the better part of the day and never lets go of her caretaker's hand.

Will I attend her birthday? No. When did I last see her? Decades ago. Will I visit her? Never. Not even at her funeral.

ILLUSTRATOR'S NOTE

*Mother and child or —The **Red Queen** and
her captive subject!*

*Bouncing physically and emotionally between
a loving father and a cold controlling mother—
where do you finally land?*

"His lot in life improved."

CHAPTER 12

REDEMPTION

IT WAS ALMOST six in the evening as he stared out of the large bay window of his sons' 34th-floor suite in Essex House. Central Park sprawled beneath him.

As the sun set on the park, it too was setting on the penultimate day of their Christmas sojourn in Manhattan. The trees turned copper under the fading sun. Skaters traversed the large ice rink, some gracefully, a few timidly, holding on to each other, while one dared to execute a salchow jump in a secluded corner.

His bird's eye view of matchstick men parading the park or clustered around a cafe, gave an impression of walking into a museum of paintings by L.S. Lowry. If he could have peered at the gathering through binoculars, it would have turned into a winter scene by Bruegel with the same air of pleasure and bonhomie.

He snuggled down on the oversized sofa swaddled in thick fleecy blankets his head on a large fluffy pillow, reading, then gently succumbed to sleep.

"Pops, wake up! It's almost nine!" Chris exhorted. "We have to go. They'll be closing off Times Square soon for New Year's."

Observing his wife grimacing, he charged to her rescue. "You go with your brother," he answered. "It's too cold for us. We'll watch the fireworks from here."

Alex entered the room. "Pops, we're hungry. Can we order room service?"

"You must be kidding. Do you know how expensive that is? AND there's a 20% charge before tip to boot. No thank you. How about pizza? There's an Italian takeout behind our hotel." He yawned and stretched. "I'll go if you like. It'll be a lot quicker than ordering. What do you fancy?"

Having got his marching orders, he put on his arctic outerwear and proceeded to the elevator.

Whereas exiting the front entrance of the Essex filled you with awe at the vista of Central Park across the avenue, the back entrance deposited you onto a narrow street the size of an alleyway. The pizza joint awaited him. He rotated through the revolving door, holding his breath to fit, and walked straight into blinding snow. Disoriented, he stumbled into a police motorbike, the size and build of a mini tank. To his amazement, the whole street was lined with police bikes. There must have been hundreds of them—as far as the eye could see—all parked at an angle within inches of each other. He squeezed through a gap between them, praying he wouldn't knock one over causing a domino effect of fallen and crumpled motorbikes. Finding his balance, he zigzagged his way across the street.

Portabella hadn't the room to swing a cat. A foot-wide, stand-up, shelf across the window acted as its only table. To have two customers in there would have been a crowd. The place was packed with close to fifty policemen. For a minute, he thought he had stepped into an episode of The Simpsons. The cops, all outfitted with large, gold-rimmed sunglasses appeared piled on top of each other. They were so burly that he couldn't understand why their uniforms hadn't burst, let alone how each had managed to negotiate an entrance that barely allowed his five-foot-four frame to pass.

The welcoming smell of baking bread, garlic, and sizzling meat restored his sense of well-being.

"A large Hawaiian and a large Meat Lovers, please. And a large Coke," he said when it was finally his turn to order. An 18" fully loaded pizza for $20. Not bad in the heart of New York.

"It'll take half an hour. We're really busy."

He was sure there were a dozen cops ahead of him.

What was he to do in the meantime? Walk this narrow alley-way? In the darkness outside, thick snow muffled the streetlights like a scene out of a foggy Victorian London. Pedestrians scuttled from one shelter to the next, on their way to Times Square to glimpse a sight of the Waterford Crystal ball about to drop from the roof of a nearby skyscraper. If he retreated home now, he would never want to come back. In answer to his dilemma, two policemen vacated the stand-up table. He occupied the spot immediately, breathing a sigh of relief.

He leaned forward on the shelf, almost touching the misted window, and gusts of cold air attacked him every time the door opened. Periodically, he wiped away the mist in front of him with a discarded paper napkin and stared out at the miserable weather.

This was precisely why he didn't want to come to New York in the first place. It reminded him of his first winter in Canada when, his instinct was to pack his bags and return to England on the next flight.

His mother's words echoed through his mind. "Calgary? Where's that? You're in London holding a well-paid job. Why leave for a hole-in-the-wall cowtown? What a waste!" His friends and colleagues had said the same.

Suddenly, a spectre appeared before him of the octogenarian who served him behind the counter at Petrossian. He re-lived her infectious smile, despite her kyphosis forcing her to permanently bend forward and the vivid Versace blouse she sported with such obvious pleasure. He remembered the "gift of the Magi"—a Gund bear from the walk-in safe in the nether recesses of Bloomingdale's and his joy at retrieving first edition copies of Hyman Kaplan he had to leave behind in East Africa.

In truth, he had never wanted to go to England either, but his English family—the Asletts—who looked after him as his mother couldn't, loved him more than their own. Yet, his mind, given the slightest opportunity to roam, wandered back, time and time again, to his home in Africa. What did he miss the most? To belong. To be accepted unconditionally.

He never had the chance to thank the tough-talking Manhattan bus driver who wouldn't take cash and showered his family with timetables and route maps, even making an unscheduled stop in front of Grand Central Station to save them a walk in the unforgiving snowstorm. This went beyond the practise of hospitality. It was as though, in that one moment of time, the driver had suddenly connected with these foreign, bedraggled water rats and treated them as she would've her own family or friends.

Unquestionably, she made him think of an equally overweight, initially grumpy and intimidating partner of the Canadian firm that hired him from England. The outwardly hide-bound partner had, against all expectations, stooped his six-foot-six frame to participate in completing an all-red jigsaw puzzle with him, thus cementing a bond of solidarity and friendship.

Sitting here in a Manhattan pizza parlour, constantly de-misting the window to witness the mayhem of a frigid winter outside, he realized it wasn't the balmy weather of Africa or the Bahamas at Christmas he missed. It was the welcoming arms of a community.

A decade after he moved to Calgary, he was returning from Los Angeles from yet another Christmas holiday. As he looked down from his cabin window, he sighed to himself.

"Home at last."

That's when he understood.

Calgarians didn't notice his colour or pedigree, nor did they practise the manners of hypocrisy against him that he witnessed in England, when away from the hearth and home of the Asletts. Calgarians judged others by their character and actions. You were rewarded for your contribution to society not for the impeccable accent you cultivated. And why shouldn't they do so?

They were, in the majority, recent immigrants, all trying their best to make their own way. Calgarians may have been gentler in manner than their New York counterparts, but to him and his family, New Yorkers, beneath their gruffness, showed them exemplary hospitality.

Many years ago, in Calgary, while he was still young and single, a friend took him to a town hall meeting held by The Forum Group. The pitch was directed to those dissatisfied with themselves and their environment. For $600, they promised you a weekend course to turn your life around.

The facilitator, uncannily dressed like a Mormon in a smart black suit and tie, addressed the audience from his lectern. With a beaming smile, he asked, "How many of you have dared to follow your dream? Have dared to unleash the amazing potential within?" The question must have been rhetorical as the facilitator continued for a further fifteen minutes before he stopped.

At the end of his speech, he waited for someone to put their hand up.

Fed up with the man's smug and condescending manner and noticing no response from the rest of the audience, he raised his hand.

"I have," he said. "And I wish I never had. I failed at everything. Almost went bankrupt several times and am still paying off the debts I incurred. I should never have unleashed the potential I wrongly thought I had."

A hush descended upon the room. Someone in the back attempted a desultory clap before being silenced. The facilitator's smile froze as he asked someone to respond. No one did.

While working at his first job in Calgary, he began to trade in gold futures. He failed, racking up a debt half the size of his annual salary. He shifted to stock trading, investing heavily then went down in financial flames when the recession hit.

Squinting through the rapidly misting windows of Portabella, he analysed each deal he had failed in as objectively as he could. With hindsight, each had the potential of making him a millionaire overnight. But the chances were less than one half of one percent. The ultra-high-risk investments he enthusiastically participated in had a 99% chance of failing, each time burdening him with insurmountable debt. After years in a well-paying profession, all he possessed was a sleeping bag in a rented bachelor suite. Why did he do this to himself time and time again? As an accountant, shouldn't he, of all people, have known better?

During all this time, he had been in a four-year social relationship with a Muslim Ismaili girl. Being an Ismaili, with four strapping, traditionally-minded brothers meant he had to follow a specific code of conduct. From both sides, particularly from his mother, there was considerable pressure put on him to marry as soon as possible. His girlfriend was a professional accountant, a Pukkah Ismaili and showed all due deference to his mother.

But how could they marry when they had endless arguments? To him, she was extremely controlling (much to his mother's liking) demanding daily attendance at their mosque. They would fight, split up, then return, treading the same mill over and over again.

Through sympathetic friends, he found a counsellor and invited his girlfriend to attend. She came once, then never again. It was the last time he saw her.

He continued the sessions for nine months.

The counsellor was petite like his mother. She also wore her hair in a bun and always dressed immaculately, her back, ramrod straight. She was an ardent follower of Joseph Campbell, the father of the theory of family mythologies.

"Imagine you were your father at your age now. What would be your concerns? Imagine you were your grandfather at your age. What would be your concerns?"

"How do I know? My grandfather died when I was four."

She gave him a look that shrivelled all resistance and continued asking questions.

Once the answers were written down, it was curious how simple the thread was that ran through them. The family myth mirrored was the same for both his families despite the disparity in their geography and culture.

Both families struggled to survive, barely keeping their head above water. Later, as the counselling progressed, he understood that, subconsciously, he carried profound guilt in having a well-paid job and living a life of comfort so far above that of mere survival. The almost fanatical lack of furniture, the use of a sleeping bag provided a path back to living in survival mode. The investing in high risk-taking ventures was a subconscious desire to force himself into constant high debt to struggle as both his families had from one generation to another.

What of choosing girlfriends with whom he would constantly fight for an equal share of power and acceptance? It was to win his Indian mother's love back, reliving the old battles with her, now he was an adult with more power than he ever had when facing her as a child.

No matter the hocus-pocus conclusion, he began to adhere to a strict financial policy of low to no risk, rather than concentrate on the lottery chance of hitting a jackpot. His lot in life improved. He analysed each encounter with a female in the same light, sifting away troubled characters, saving so much time and stress. The sessions taught him the art of patience and the confidence to believe in his future.

"Pizzas up," the Italian-Brooklyn accented exclamation recalled him to the present.

He left, trampling the snow-covered street like a drunken sailor on his way back to his ship, the bag containing the Coke swinging haphazardly from side-to-side, while his hands tightly clutched the two large pizzas. His glasses steamed up then iced-over as he faced the hurdle of police bikes again with growing trepidation.

Arriving back at Essex House, the boys munched through their pizzas, guzzling down tumblers of Coke before disappearing down the corridor and out. Their mother's voice rang after them. "Don't forget your gloves."

Kids off on their own, husband and wife huddled together under warm fleecy blankets, resting their heads on oversized, down-filled pillows, patiently awaiting the fireworks.

He had found a local FM radio station broadcasting classical music. Elgar's *Nimrod* began its ascent. Out of the corner of his eyes, he gazed at Laura in awe. They had been married twenty-three years.

"You watch. Your marriage won't last six months," his Mum had said. Yet, here they were, still hand in hand, with two boys ready to conquer the world.

His thoughts intermingled with the music, his mind like Elgar's, reflecting on what had been, what could have been, and what was now.

AUTHOR'S NOTE

With Gratitude and Disbelief

*Witnessing the ravages of time on those around me:
death, illness, dementia, divorce, addiction, disharmony
in marriage I thank the gods for delivering
me safely home.*

ILLUSTRATOR'S NOTE

*Celebrating a new year and a new life—letting go of
the weight of the past and coming full circle to a better
understanding for where he's been and
gratitude for where he is now!*

—THE END—

THE AUTHOR
Emil Rem

I WAS BORN in 1955 in Tanzania to East Indian, Muslim parents. My mother, who possessed no education but held impossible ambitions, divorced my father when I was five and was immediately ostracized by her community. She moved to England and took me with her. The only work she could get was as a trainee nurse, and she found she couldn't look after me. An English working class family volunteered to take me in until she could find a permanent home for me. The initial two weeks turned into 12 years before my mother took me away from them.

Father continued to work for an airline which permitted me to travel free on standby. Initially, the tickets were for visiting home every holiday I had. From the age of 12, I began to travel the world on my own. Neither of my parents could afford to come with me. My mother gave me a pittance for my travels—it was all she could afford. I would arrive at London airport with a carry-on bag and a wad of tickets and take whichever airline had space available. I could be in Moscow or Rio De Janiero, I never knew. Nor did my family.

With enough money to last me a week, I had little choice—either talk to the passengers and have them invite me to stay with them or sleep on the airport floor and walk to town and back. There were no guide books. I walked and walked until my thighs came to look like slabs of ham.

Travelling to Africa, I saw the gradual disintegration of my community as each country gained its independence.

In 1970, Idi Amin threw out our community overnight in Uganda and other countries followed suit, nationalizing businesses and property.

In England, my English family gave me a St. Christopher's Cross to protect me in my travels. Reaching Africa, the cross was replaced by a green armband of cotton thread and a Muslim missionary hired to knock some religion into me. But the harm had already been done. In England, the combination of school and joining the cubs for Sunday church, led me to fall in love with hymns and psalms and the beauty of prose in the St. James' version of the Bible. That, the learning of Christmas carols for the school play, and my teacher's Friday readings of *The Adventures of Tom Sawyer* or *Wind in the Willows*, brought on the love of literature. Books were an escape from the misery and solitude. Apart from my English family, they were the only stability in my life.

To spite my Indian mother who was always hovering around me demanding the best from me, I failed my exams and sped headlong into accounting to escape my mother's wrath and the threat to retake my final years at school.

My accounting qualification allowed me to make a new home in Calgary, Canada where I became a scourge to my employers—they found I couldn't add!

In Calgary, much to the distress of my mother, I married a Filipina who bore me two boys within 21 months of each other. By mutual assent, both boys became Roman Catholic—leading my mother to disinherit me.

My mother had always discouraged me from writing or anything creative—there was no money in it. It was not until little by little, as I heard of the death of 'this family member' or 'that close family friend', that the thought came to me to preserve these memories for my boys. My final decesion was precipitated by the death of my father. He had joined us in Calgary several years earlier and was beloved both by my wife and children.

THE TEAM...

LORIE MILLER HANSEN

I have been a professional graphic designer for over twenty years—but more importantly, I've been an illustrator my entire life. I began at the age of two, with an ink portrait of my mother on the front page of a very *very* expensive book.

For someone whose passion is expression through art and creative design, being given the opportunity to work on *Heart of New York* has been one of the highlights of my career.

My first drawing—I think Mom was impressed!

ANDREA CINNAMOND

In my former life I was a high-tech scientist, but when I discovered the 'techy' online world—where I could play at the intersection of logic and creativity—I was hooked.

One of my many areas of expertise is the building and implementation of digital (ePub) books and I love nothing more (*other than my three teenagers and our cat Amesbury!*) than working with and supporting motivated, inspired writers and creatives. Working on *Heart of New York* has been an amazing project that employs all the things I love to do.

ROBIN van ECK

I am an editor and author of literary, contemporary, horror and weird, offbeat and creative nonfiction. *Heart of New York,* in its way, fits into all of those categories! It has been a wonderful project—one that has called on all of my editing skills.

Made in the USA
Middletown, DE
29 October 2022

13751000R00106